GETTING STARTED:

An Overview of School Development Practices

Edited by
Kathleen C. Collins, SFCC, M.B.A.

Department of Elementary Schools
National Catholic Educational Association

ISBN 1-55833-183-2

Contents

Foreword

Why do we need another book on development?

In 1990, the American Catholic Bishops issued their statement *Support for Catholic Schools.* In it they set for themselves four goals; one of these states, "New initiatives will be launched to secure sufficient assistance from both the private and public sectors for Catholic parents to exercise this right [of sending their children to Catholic schools]." A year later, 250 delegates representing all members of the Catholic school community met in Washington, D.C., at the National Congress on Catholic Schools for the 21st Century. One of the directional statements passed by the assembly stated, "We will implement and evaluate comprehensive development programs at the local, diocesan and national level."

What steps are being taken to achieve these goals? The NCEA report *Balance Sheet for Catholic Elementary Schools: 1995 Income and Expenses* (Kealey, 1996) provides some insight into answering this question. During the 1994-95 school year, 15 percent of the elementary schools surveyed reported that they had a development director, although only 32 percent of these schools had a full-time development director. Only 40 percent of the schools had endowment programs. A little over one percent of the per-pupil cost came from endowment programs. Almost 85 percent of the per-pupil cost came from tuition and a parish subsidy. During the past eight years, NCEA's Department of Elementary Schools has provided the Development Training Program to over 800 schools/parishes. This leaves about 6,200 schools without this training to establish comprehensive development programs.

The data suggest that much more needs to be done to get more Catholic schools involved in comprehensive development efforts. Thus, the need for this book is very clear.

The authors of the various chapters of this book are all involved in development activities. They write from their firsthand experience. They are part of the small but highly successful group of schools that have comprehensive development efforts. They wish to share their experiences with you and to encourage you to get started. While we look hopefully to some form of government assistance to parents so they can exercise their constitutional right of sending their children to the school of their choice, development efforts are absolutely essential in the intervening years and will always be necessary.

The Department of Elementary Schools expresses its gratitude to Sister Kass Collins for bringing together the authors for this book, to the authors for sharing their ideas, to its own Tara McCallum for proofreading and editing the manuscript, and to NCEA's Tia Gray and Beatriz Ruiz for designing the cover and layout. The department offers this book to its members with the hope that the easy-to-follow steps presented will encourage more schools to undertake comprehensive development activities to ensure the continuation and expansion of quality American Catholic Schools for the 21st Century.

Feast of the Birth of Mary, 1996

Kieran Hartigan, RSM, P.D.
President

Robert J. Kealey, Ed.D.
Executive Director

Department of Elementary Schools
National Catholic Educational Association

CHAPTER 1:
DEVELOPMENT VS. FUND-RAISING

Kathleen C. Collins, SFCC

This chapter will answer these questions:
1. What is fund-raising?
2. What is development?
3. What is the basic approach to each?
4. What are some examples of each?
5. What are some results if a school continues to do fund-raising only?
6. What are some results to expect if a school begins to do development?
7. How does a school, a principal, a school board start the initial steps?

1. What is fund-raising?

Candy bars, wrapping paper, magazines—you name it, and Catholic schools have sold it to make a profit to meet school expenses. It seems this type of fund-raising has been a part of school life forever. In recent years, schools have added socials, lotteries, selling of scrip, etc. Although many of these activities are very time-consuming and to some may not seem appropriate for a Catholic school, they do generate substantial funds. Even prestigious colleges and universities sell a variety of products with their name on them; this is fund-raising. Because of the substantial income generated, fund-raising will probably continue to be part of the school scene for the immediate future.

2. What is development?

Development, on the other hand, is a fairly recent phenomenon within Catholic elementary and secondary schools. Some colleges and universities have had annual giving programs since the early 1900s, while the mid-1940s saw practically all institutions of higher learning establishing development programs. Development is concerned with establishing a strategic plan, improving the public relations of the school, marketing it, recruiting and retaining students, and securing support for the school in terms of human and financial resources. Development is much more comprehensive than fund-raising.

3. What is the basic approach to each?

The basic approach and concepts of development and fund-raising differ greatly. Panic reactions to negative immediate deficits sometimes start the process of fund-raising, but it takes the commitment of the principal and school board to foster a strong development effort that looks hopefully to the future.

Terms such as *crisis orientation*; *temporary solutions*; *limited, short-range objectives*; *Band-Aid approach*; and *negotiating from a position of weakness* are associated with fund-raising. Fund-raising will always be a necessity, but development offers a long-term solution to a school's financial stability.

Development fosters terms such as *complete integrity, long-range planning, public relations, positive attitudes, good business management,* and *substantial investments.*

4. What are some examples of each?

When you look at the types of activities employed in fund-raising and in development, you immediately see a striking difference between the two:

DEVELOPMENT	FUND-RAISING
Endowment fund	Bingo
Estate planning	Car wash
Annuity programs	Annual bazaar
Business and industry grants	$10-a-plate dinner
Major gift prospects	Festival
Wills clinics	Magazine sales
Proposals to foundations	Las Vegas night

5. What are some results if a school continues to do fund-raising only?

Fund-raising is only a stopgap measure. It may keep a school going for a while, but the results alone are not sufficient to assure a school's survival for the future. Development has to do with long-range planning. It starts with the premise that the school will be here 5 or 10 or 50 years from now and sets in motion a series of activities that will lead to a secure and successful future. If you think your school is worth saving for the future, fund-raising alone will not get it there.

6. What are some results to expect if a school begins to do development?

A mature development effort, on the other hand, receives large private donations on a consistent annual basis, has money programmed for 5 to 10 years down the road, works from a clearly projected long-range plan, reports progress to all publics on an annual basis, and generates private dollars from sources such as insurance policies and foundation grants.

7. How does a school, a principal, a school board start the initial steps?

The above paragraph talks about a mature development effort. If you have purchased this book, it is assumed you already know that development is the avenue of choice. Read on, now, to learn how to establish a development program in your school.

(Sister Kathleen C. Collins, SFCC, is the associate executive director for planning and development of the NCEA Department of Elementary Schools.)

Additional Reading on the Topic from NCEA

Kealey, Robert J. (1996). *Balance Sheet for Catholic Elementary Schools: 1995 Income and Expenses.*

Kealey, Robert J., and Collins, Kathleen C. (1994). *Stewardship and the Catholic School Tuition Program.*

Konsen, Joel M. (1991). *The Role of the Principal in Development.*

CHAPTER 2:
SCHOOL DEVELOPMENT COMMITTEE

John Burke

This chapter will answer these questions:

1. What is a school development committee?
2. How does a school development committee help the school?
3. What types of people should be on a school development committee?
4. How does a school select members for its school development committee?
5. What is the most effective use of a school development committee?
6. How does a school development committee evaluate itself?

1.   What is a school development committee?

A school development committee is a group of dynamic, committed, and talented people who understand and believe in the philosophy and mission of the school. The group's involvement of their wisdom, time, work, and wealth will advance the present and future goals, programs, facilities and financial stability of the school. The committee is a non-policy-making group whose sole purpose is to increase support for the school. Some of the literature on school development talks about the *school development board* or the *development council*. In this text, the term *school development committee* will be used.

2.   How does a school development committee help the school?

An effective school development committee enjoys the challenge of meeting the needs of the school and can assist the school in at least seven ways:

- Committee members have the ability to assist your school now and to insure its financial stability for the future.
- The members' successful career experiences can assist in efforts to "market the school."
- The committee members possess a network of friends and business associates who will assist their efforts to support your school.
- The committee members possess the varied skills necessary to execute highly successful development efforts.
- The members have within their businesses, or have the ability to acquire, personnel, building, and financial resources to assist you and your volunteers.
- Some of the members will have experience in managerial and fiscal matters that can be a great asset for the school.
- The reputation of committee members enhances the credibility of the school.

3. What types of people should be on a school development committee?

The best people you can find for your committee are highly successful salespeople, public relations or advertising executives, construction company owners, restaurant owners, bank or finance executives, and others who are well respected in the community. On the top of the list also are foundation executives, real-estate executives, funeral home directors, lawyers, CEOs or senior vice presidents, and high school or college development officers.

4. How does a school select members for its school development committee?

A good beginning step for you to take is to form a search committee to recommend candidates for the school development committee. You want to exercise caution by not automatically filling the development committee with dedicated home and school officers. Though a few of these people may join the committee, an effective school development committee demands people with varied experiences, wealth, and many contacts.

The search committee to suggest possible candidates to the school development committee should consist of the pastor, former pastors, parish priests, the principal, former principals, long-time parishioners, present and past faculty, interested alumni, and some dedicated volunteers. The types of people the search committee should consider are successful alumni, parents and grandparents of students and graduates, former teachers who are now involved in business or school administration, business leaders interested in educational reform, vendors of the school and parish, and community leaders. (See Worksheet 2.1 at the end of this chapter for a sample form to use.) If you are fortunate enough to have locally based philanthropists, invite them to participate. Generous donors to the school and parish are a must to get involved in your development committee.

After listing names of possible candidates, the committee should attempt to research the background of the candidates. Hopefully, the list reflects a diversity of gender, ethnicity, locality, and career types. No development committee needs three lawyers, all males, or everyone from one ethnic group. Since you will want to involve your committee members when requesting grants, it is helpful to have a diverse group.

Keep in mind that you are looking for ideal school development committee members, people of position and wealth with many contacts. Check out the history of their giving and the personal wealth of each candidate. You need to know if the candidate is in a management position in a corporation or is a sole-proprietor business leader. You may wish to personally meet some possible candidates to get a feel for them. The focus of such a visit is merely to explore ways the person might help the school. See if you can find out if he or she has a network of friends and business associates. A primary requisite, of course, is professional expertise and a degree of involvement in other causes, especially in church and education. People who previously were not involved in philanthropy, however, can become wonderful development committee members when the invitation or need is right. As with everything in life, people can grow in commitment of time, talents, and treasure.

What if the search committee does not come up with a large number of candidates? Begin your school development activities even if you come up with five or six people. These members of the committee, once they see the importance of their task, may recommend others to join.

Having completed the research on the candidates and formulated a list of people to be invited to become part of the school development committee, the principal or pastor or both should meet face-to-face with each candidate to extend the invitation. Position the invitation as an honor to the potential committee member, not as a potential financial burden. Many business executives need to improve their community involvement and outreach for various business reasons; serving on the school development committee provides this community involvement. A lunch with the candidate is an excellent opportunity to explain the role and expectations of membership. If lunch cannot be arranged, try to have some personal meeting with the person, even if it is brief. If this is impossible, a warm letter citing reasons for selection followed by a phone call is effective. A sample letter of invitation is presented below. Even if the candidates recommended by the search committee refuse, they will feel honored to have been chosen for consideration.

SAMPLE LETTER OF INVITATION

Dear_____:

   It is with joyous anticipation and with strong confidence in our present mission and future visions that we are planning to inaugurate a development committee here at St. Thomas Elementary School. This committee, comprised of 15 members, hopefully will invest time, talents, and treasure in our present and future students. Having researched these candidates, we believe that we have found the kind of generous, talented, and dedicated people who would do any committee proud.

   Father Ryan, our pastor, and I would like the opportunity to talk to you about becoming a member of our development committee. Your history of service to St. Thomas makes you an obvious choice. I will call you next week to set up an appointment for lunch so that we might discuss what membership entails.

Sincerely,

Principal

   When offering committee membership to a candidate, the first group of topics to cover deals with the school. Provide an overview of the school and its program. If you have literature about the school (school brochure, alumni newsletter, yearbook, etc.), leave it with the person. Mention why the school needs a development committee. Share the vision for the future of the school as clearly and dramatically as possible.

   The second group of topics concerns the time commitment of the person. Mention the number of committee meetings set up for the year. The number is usually from a minimum of 4 to a maximum of 10. Summers are generally free of meetings. Indicate the time when these meetings are generally held. State the subcommittee work that may be required. If the members of the committee have a term, mention that this period is three or six years. Also indicate if the person can serve a second term.

   The third group of topics to cover concerns the personal commitment of the person. If the candidate possesses a particular skill, ask if he or she is willing to serve the committee in that capacity. This can be a very flattering way to approach this person's recruitment. State the amount of financial commitment expected either through personal donations or through personal solicitation of others. Although every school and community are different, I would recommend $5,000 as a minimum figure that is expected. Hopefully, many on the committee can raise significantly more.

   Finally, share the names of other school development committee members who have already accepted and the number of committee members you want to recruit. Some people respond very favorably when they know the company that they will be keeping. Promise to provide the inservice necessary for the committee to function well. Invite the candidate to suggest items to be included in the inservice sessions. Try not to underplay involvement; successful people love challenges. Answer all questions as honestly as you can.

Once the candidates have been chosen and have accepted positions, the principal or development director should be ready to provide the inservice program promised to the committee members. The principal should know the basic philosophy and framework of a development program. The administrator needs this background information to decide what topics are needed to begin inservice work. It would be most helpful for the principal to attend a comprehensive development workshop. Conferencing with principals who have effective development programs in their schools will prove enlightening. A development consultant who comes recommended by other schools would probably be a good choice to lead these inservice sessions.

The inservice leader should begin by explaining the role of the committee, clarifying that a school development committee is not a policy-making group like a board of trustees or school board. Clearly, the function of the members of the school development committee is to give and get! The principal or development director should explain how development differs from traditional fundraising. The committee should understand the comprehensiveness of a development program. Familiarizing the committee with the essential parts of the school's long-range strategic plan can lead it to construct its first-year plan as soon as possible. Sending the committee members to a comprehensive professional development workshop for several days is an excellent form of inservice for those schools that can afford it and the people who can afford to give their time to it.

5. What is the most effective use of a school development committee?

Every school development committee has to decide which areas of development it will target. This decision is predicated largely on whether the school has a full-time development director, the degree of involvement of the school administration, the number of volunteers available, and whether the school has an active alumni association.

In some instances, the development committee does all facets of development work. Where there is a fully staffed development office, the committee can limit itself to making generous contributions of time, talents, and resources and to soliciting donors for major gifts. The following is only a sampling of areas of involvement for the committee:

- Sponsoring and organizing special events like dinners, golf days, cruises, and concerts
- Soliciting major gifts for capital campaign and annual funds
- Executing a planned giving program involving themselves, friends, parishioners, and business associates
- Using influence to secure foundation, government, and corporate grants
- Lending marketing expertise to school recruitment programs
- Developing student tuition grants programs
- Participating in mail solicitation and phonathons for the annual appeal

This list of suggested activities should help the school development committee plan strategically for the future. In addition to their personal involvement, some school development committee members, because of their position in a company, are able to "lend" the school clerical and telephone assistance, furniture, space, and personnel to execute many facets of the development program. Clearly, the school administration will become aware of these resources by asking development committee members what they can contribute rather than passively waiting for such offers of assistance.

6. How does a school development committee evaluate itself?

The school development committee, its various subcommittees, and individual members should set goals for themselves. Having these goals greatly simplifies the end-of-year evaluations. The evaluation process should take place both on an individual and a group basis. The evaluation can be done by the principal or the chairperson of the development committee or a small committee. Clearly, a committee member who misses meetings or fails to carry out individual responsibilities must be notified and be removed if he or she fails to improve after being notified. A member who is not accomplishing his or her assigned tasks can have a negative effect on all other committee members.

Evaluation should also take the form of internal and external processes. Internally, certain goals stated at the beginning of the school year can be evaluated easily. Much harder to evaluate is the quality of the work. Some schools find it helpful to have a development professional look at the program from the viewpoint of an objective outsider. This process is known as a development audit.

The evaluators review the one-year plan and the strategic three-year plan. The evaluators determine whether the program is on target with regard to time, achievement of goals, and new monies acquired. Answers and plans for correcting shortfalls must be addressed during the evaluation process. These provide the school development committee with valuable data which will lead to increased or decreased activities.

Evaluation generally gives the committee, the donors, and the school family a document which makes everyone feel proud and grateful. Philanthropy should make people feel good and provide motivation for the staff to improve the quality of instruction.

Summary

A school development committee can be one of the greatest assets a school has. Across the country, such committees raise millions of dollars. These dedicated philanthropists have added quality Catholic education to the list of their myriad interests. In addition to the money raised, development committee members offer fiscal advice, public relations skills, marketing techniques, and a simple business approach to the schools they serve.

Hopefully, Catholic school administrators will reach out and ask these wonderful people to invest their wealth, wisdom, and work for the students presently in the schools and those who will be coming in the third millennium.

(John Burke, M.S., is principal of St. Thomas Aquinas Elementary School in the Bronx, N.Y.)

Additional Reading on the Topic from NCEA

LaRiviere, Ann. (1993). *The Development Council: Cornerstone for Success.*

Stangle, Anita. (1990). *The One-Person Development Office.*

WORKSHEET 2.1

Whom Do We Know?

Ask the search committee members to share the names of people who might serve on the development committee, such as parishioners, alumni, and community leaders.

Successful salespersons   _____

Successful public relations,
  advertising executives   _____

Construction company owners   _____

Restaurant owners   _____

Bank or finance executives   _____

Real-estate executives   _____

Funeral home directors   _____

Lawyers   _____

Corporation CEOs   _____

Senior vice presidents   _____

High school, college development
  officer or administrator   _____

Community leaders   _____

Talented faculty members   _____

Foundation executives   _____

Media, sports celebrities   _____

CHAPTER 3:
STRATEGIC PLANNING

Jean Wincek, CSJ

This chapter will answer these questions:

1. What is strategic planning?
2. What are the steps in the planning process?
3. Who is responsible for initiating the planning process?
4. How do you begin the process?
5. What contextual and internal elements need to be addressed?
6. How does the committee develop the plan?
7. What goes into the draft and refinement of the plan?
8. How does the principal carry out the implementation of the plan?
9. How is the plan updated?

1. What is strategic planning?

The concept of strategic planning is somewhat abstract. It is an attempt to answer the questions: Where are we now? Where do we want to be? How will we get there? Who will go with us? How much will it cost?

Planning is a process of assigning the school's resources (people, time, finances, etc.) to achieve the school's mission.

2. What are the steps in the planning process?

There are six phases or steps in the planning process:
- Initiating the planning process
- Considering contextual and internal elements
- Developing the strategic plan
- Drafting and refining the plan
- Designing and carrying out the implementation strategies
- Updating the plan on an annual basis

3. Who is responsible for initiating the planning process?

The pastor, principal, and school board decide if the timing is right to initiate the planning process and what their roles will be. Once the commitment to do the planning is made, then they decide what *long-range* means—three years? five years? longer?—and who will chair the planning committee.

4. How do you begin the process?

Once the decision is made to do the planning, then—
- Construct a timetable and calendar of meetings
- Determine where meetings will be held
- Determine if a consultant is needed or desirable
- Consider what expenses might be involved in doing the planning

- Decide on the size of the planning committee and what constituencies should be represented
- Suggest names of potential committee members (See Worksheet 3.1 at the end of this chapter for a sample form to use.)
- Determine what background material (e.g., mission statement and philosophy of the school, financial and enrollment data, trends in education) is needed prior to the study and who will prepare it (Worksheet 3.2 through Worksheet 3.6 at the end of this chapter are sample forms to use.)

5. What contextual and internal elements need to be addressed?

The strategic long-range planning committee—

- Reviews the history of the school, its current situation, and its role in the community
- Reviews the mission and philosophy of the school and decides if they are clear or need to be changed
- Brainstorms external factors that may impinge upon or enhance the school, e.g., a new home development in the area
- Brainstorms internal issues the school may face, e.g., the religious community's decision to withdraw from the school
- Determines critical issues the school may face, based on external factors and internal issues

6. How does the committee develop the plan?

Once the above issues have been addressed, the planning committee comes to a consensus on goals for the future of the school. Each area of school life (curriculum, staffing, building, enrollment, finances, development) will have strategies to meet the goals. Those strategies need to be prioritized. Finally, the committee determines the format for the plan and commissions a writing team to draft preliminary goals and suggestions for implementation.

7. What goes into the draft and refinement of the plan?

Now the planning committee reviews the mission and educational philosophy of the school in light of the proposed plan, decides how to review the plan and how to test the feasibility and desirability of the preferred scenario and goals with various stakeholders, edits and refines the draft of the plan, and presents it to the board for approval. It is certainly appropriate for the committee to celebrate and ritualize the conclusion of these phases of the work.

8. How does the principal carry out the implementation of the plan?

The principal, in consultation with those involved in the implementation process and, where appropriate, with board approval—

- Plans the implementation program, including actions to be taken; who is responsible; beginning, completion, and reporting dates; and required resources
- Incorporates into the annual budget funds to implement the plan
- Includes implementation of the program in the principal's and board's yearly goals
- Monitors the progress of the plan through reports to the board at regular intervals
- Adjusts the implementation program, as necessary

See Worksheet 3.7 at the end of this chapter for a sample form to use.

9. How is the plan updated?

The principal, with appropriate groups, including the school board—

- Reviews external factors, internal issues, and critical issues

- Reviews strategic priorities
- Revises the plan and implementation program, based on new information
- Includes revisions in the coming year's operational planning

The following worksheets in this chapter are adapted from *Taking Hold of the Future: The ABC's of Strategic Planning*.

(Sister Jean Wincek, CSJ, Ed.D., is a consultant for EXCEL, Inc., based in Chicago and an adjunct instructor at St. Mary's College of Minnesota and the University of St. Thomas, also in Minnesota.)

Additional Reading on the Topic from NCEA

Wincek, Jean, and O'Malley, Colleen. (1995). *Taking Hold of the Future: The ABC's of Strategic Planning*.

WORKSHEET 3.1

Potential Members of the
Strategic Long-range Planning Committee

Directions: Please suggest members to serve on the strategic long-range planning committee by completing the form below.

Name	Background and Skills	Invite Yes/No	Accept Yes/No
1.			
2.			
3.			
4.			
5.			
6.			
7.			
8.			
9.			
10.			

WORKSHEET 3.2

Background Materials
Enrollment Statistics

	Year					
Grade	1991-92	1992-93	1993-94	1994-95	1995-96	1996-97
Infant						
Pre-K 3						
Pre-K 4						
K						
1						
2						
3						
4						
5						
6						
7						
8						
Total						

WORKSHEET 3.3

Background Materials
Enrollment Projections

The following pages describe a way to project enrollment for the next five years. This is a three-step process. These statistics indicate what enrollment trends may be if current trends continue without any internal or external intervening factors.

Directions: Using the enrollment statistics on the preceding page, transfer the numbers from the four most recent years to the chart below.

FOUR MOST RECENT YEARS FROM ENROLLMENT STATISTICS

Year	Infant	3yr	4yr	K	1	2	3	4	5	6	7	8	Total
Year 1 1992-93													
Year 2 1993-94													
Year 3 1994-95													
Year 4 1995-96													

WORKSHEET 3.4

Background Materials
Enrollment Projections

Directions:

- To develop a five-year enrollment projection with a liberal estimate of the number of students, determine the highest number of students you might expect in your lowest grade.

- To obtain an estimate of the number of students in each grade for the next school year, multiply the actual number of students in that grade this year by the average retention ratio (see pp. 50-51 of NCEA's *Taking Hold of the Future: The ABC's of Strategic Planning*) for that grade. Put the answer in the row and column representing the year and grade for the following year.

- Fill in the chart for the next five years by multiplying each number in a column by the retention ratio average for that grade.

- Next, develop a conservative projection of enrollment by determining the smallest number of students you might expect in your lowest grade.

- Repeat the calculation process and fill in a separate chart for a conservative estimate of the number of students.

PROJECTION:
LIBERAL ESTIMATE OF FIVE-YEAR ENROLLMENT

						Grade							
Infant	3yr	4yr	K	1	2	3	4	5	6	7	8	Total

Average Retention Ratio

Year

1996-97

1997-98

1998-99

1999-2000

2000-2001

WORKSHEET 3.5

Background Materials
Enrollment Projections*

PARISHIONERS AND NONPARISHIONERS

	Year				
	1991-92	1992-93	1993-94	1994-95	1995-96
Parishioners					
Nonparishioners					
Total					

PROJECTIONS
(Using the average ratio for the last five years)

	Year				
	1996-97	1997-98	1998-99	1999-2000	2000-01
Parishioners					
Nonparishioners					
Total					

* For a detailed explanation of how to use these charts, see Appendix F in NCEA's manual *Taking Hold of the Future: The ABC's of Strategic Planning.*

WORKSHEET 3.6

Background Materials
Curriculum Changes

Below are the subjects taught in your school. List significant changes that occurred in that area under the year. These changes could include adoption of a new textbook series, staff development in the area, review of the school's resources to support the area, review of the school's philosophy and goals for teaching in the area, review of content taught in each grade.

		Year		
Curriculum Areas	**1992-93**	**1993-94**	**1994-95**	**1995-96**
Religious Studies				
Mathematics				
Reading/Literature				
Language Arts				
Social Studies				
Science				
Arts				
Others				

WORKSHEET 3.7

Implementation Form

Goal:

Implementation:

Actions	Person(s) Responsible	Start Date	Completion Date	Resources Needed	Report Date to School Board

CHAPTER 4:
VOLUNTEERS

Carol Mack

This chapter will answer these questions:

1. Why is it important to have volunteers assist the school development program?
2. What are some tasks that volunteers can do?
3. How do you recruit volunteers?
4. What positions can volunteers fill in the school development program?
5. How do you organize a volunteer handbook?
6. How do you support your volunteers?
7. What are some challenges in working with volunteers?

1. Why is it important to have volunteers assist the school development program?

A successful Catholic school development program relies on strong volunteer support. The principal and/or development professional cannot do it alone. Volunteers provide that extra set of hands to accomplish development tasks; make excellent school ambassadors to the broader community; become loyal, generous contributors; and can be relied on for their expertise and perspective. Successful volunteer programs don't just happen. They are the result of thoughtful planning and management.

In this chapter, you will learn how to solicit, use, and retain volunteers to assist in the development efforts of your school. This chapter will not discuss volunteers who assist in the academic and recreational programs of the school.

2. What are some tasks that volunteers can do?

Here are just a few ways your school can benefit from the generosity of volunteers. You need volunteers to serve as school development board members, especially if they bring with them expertise in business, financial and professional services, affluence, and influence. Volunteers are needed to do donor research; to serve as computer technicians, historians, or archivists; and to host or organize celebrations and special events. Jobs that need to be filled include phonathon callers; personal gift solicitors; and newsletter editors, writers, photographers, printers, and designers.

Enthusiastic alumni could make an alumni association a reality for your school. Stuffing, sorting, and mailing appeals and brochures need many helping hands. You might want to use a talented volunteer to do public or donor relations or to recruit other volunteers. Some volunteers who work in the business and professional communities might be willing to serve by putting you in touch with, or introducing you to, potential donors.

3. How do you recruit volunteers?

Catholic elementary schools should consider the following groups when searching for volunteers: alumni of the school, parents and grandparents of the students, parents of past students, senior citizens, friends and acquaintances of current volunteers, parishioners, and community and businesspeople. Volunteerism is an exchange relationship between the volunteer and the school; it is not a one-way gift. The volunteer contributes time, commitment, talent, and financial support in exchange for one or more of the following: friends and fellowship; a sense of belonging; a chance to gain recognition; an opportunity to learn new skills; an opportunity to establish contacts; an opportunity to effect change; a sense of responsibility; participation in the child's or grandchild's life; a need to give back something to the school.

Carefully planned recruiting is the best way to assure a successful volunteer program. Recruiting is best done face-to-face. Schools that rely on notes, newsletters, and word of mouth to recruit volunteers do not enjoy a good success rate. The following is a suggested volunteer-recruiting procedure.

Begin by making a list of the development activities you plan to undertake. Look at your list of projected development activities and then make a corresponding list of all the jobs you would like volunteers to fill. Include committee-level jobs as well as cookie-baker/coffer-maker type jobs. Write a job description for each volunteer job designation. Create a volunteer handbook containing your list of needed volunteer positions and their descriptions.

With your list of volunteer job opportunities and job descriptions in hand, network with teachers, parent organization officers, parish council members, and those who are already committed volunteers to brainstorm volunteer prospects. Your goal is to develop an exhaustive list of volunteer prospects. When the list is completed, a small group needs to suggest a particular person for a particular position. This group might include the principal, pastor, development professional, or committee chair. One by one, call the various positions and suggest names for the position. To be successful with volunteers, you have to understand that everyone's motivation is not the same. Care should be taken to fit the right volunteer with the right job. When one person has been decided upon, the group should formulate an explanation of why that person has been asked to consider accepting the job.

The best procedure is to recruit quality volunteers in person. If this is not possible, invite some by mail and follow up with a personal telephone call. Do not ask for a commitment on the phone; the person needs time to consider your offer. Follow up your phone call by sending a letter and the volunteer handbook so the potential volunteer understands the school's mission, needs, and expectations. Also send any school literature, a current newsletter, the brochure, the annual report, and news clippings. Meet with the prospect at the school to determine if his or her interests and talents mesh with the school's needs. Accept a commitment at this time and follow up with a thank-you letter and an invitation to a pre-service orientation.

The best volunteers share certain characteristics. They tend to be busy people, active in the community and other organizations. They are able to project a positive attitude and have a record of successful service. They have a connection to the school and understand and appreciate its mission.

Keep your volunteer records in a computer database with your other development records. Have the volunteer fill out a record card at the time he or she agrees to join your team. You can adapt the volunteer record card (see Worksheet 4.1 at the end of this chapter) to suit your needs. Assign a volunteer to transfer the information from the card into the computer.

4. What positions can volunteers fill in the school development program?

Although the specific volunteer needs of individual schools will differ, the examples listed below are models of the types of volunteers who are helpful to elementary school programs. In general, your program will be involved in annual fund-raising, special events, alumni and donor prospect cultivation, recruiting and retaining students, and public relations. Start by identifying prospects to chair committees who will work in these areas. These chairs become your key players along with the principal, pastor, and development director. Enlist their help to find subcommittee volunteers. Copy and fill in the list at the end of this chapter (Worksheet 4.2, List of Volunteers for the Year).

Chairperson for the Annual Fund Drive - This person will need subcommittee volunteers to coordinate personal gift solicitation, the direct mail appeal, callers for the phonathon event, and the kickoff event.

Chairperson for Public Relations and Publicity - This job is crucial to the success of any development effort. The chair will need many helping hands, however, to bring it off successfully. Committee support volunteers for this chairperson include people who will coordinate Grandparents Day, edit or write the newsletter, take photographs of events, record events for a video presentation, act as historian or archivist for the year's events, and coordinate the mailing.

Chairperson for Student Recruitment/Retention - A very important need for any school is to recruit new students and to do all you can to retain the ones you have. A person is needed to concentrate on this facet of development. This chairperson will need subcommittee volunteers to coordinate the outreach to preschoolers who are potential kindergarten and first grade students. All newly baptized babies in the school parish and feeder parishes are potential students. Their parents need to be kept informed of what is happening in the school. A volunteer could coordinate an open-house event for them and their parents. (See the NCEA publication *Letters to Parents of Preschool Children*, which contains sample letters that schools can send every six months to parents of children from birth to age 5. These explain to parents the changes that are taking place in their children and allow the school to inform the parents of its programs.) A volunteer is needed to coordinate this program for feeder parishes, and one is needed also to coordinate the annual open-house activities.

Chairperson for Special Events - Every school has special events. They are wonderful ways to get the principal, faculty, students, and staff all working on a particular project involving parents, relatives, or alumni. They offer the school a chance to attract. A volunteer chairperson takes charge of the many details and saves the school staff many hours of work. Subcommittee volunteers will give support to this chairperson by doing such things as coordinating ticket sales and refreshments.

Alumni Relations Chair - For this job, you will need the most enthusiastic alumni you can recruit. An excellent ongoing source of funding in a development effort are your alumni. They know the school and feel a lifelong loyalty for all it has done to prepare them for living. They will remember their former teachers with respect and love. This chairperson will need subcommittee volunteers to act as agents for each class. Another coordinator organizes the class reunions.

General Volunteers - Next, put together a pool of general volunteers. These are the people who say, "I don't want to be in charge, but I'll help you out. Just call me." This is the pool your chairs and coordinators can call on when they have a specific activity planned. These people are valuable resources: graphic design artists, hosts for small meetings, initiators of a phone information chain, word processors, cooks/bakers, envelope stuffers or sorters, computer gurus, and secretaries.

5. How do you organize a volunteer handbook?

A volunteer handbook is a collection of all the information necessary for your volunteers to feel informed and confident. It conveys the impression that the school is well organized, that there is a genuine need for the volunteers, and that the volunteers will make an important contribution to the success of the school as a whole.

It is best to assemble the handbook in a loose-leaf binder or pocket folder to make updating and changing easier. Office supply stores carry inexpensive three-ring binders with clear vinyl pockets on the front, allowing you to personalize the book for your school. Also available is pre-punched, three-holed paper for the copier or laser printer.

Job descriptions of the various roles that volunteers will fulfill are an important element in the handbook. When writing the job description, begin with the job title and then list the responsibilities. Be sure to mention the length of term for each position, which could be the whole school year or shorter or longer, depending on the event or position. Potential volunteers will find it helpful if you can give an estimate of the time commitment, e.g., four hours a week for eight weeks. The volunteer needs to know to whom to report or whom to call if there is a problem. A good inclusion would be a chart or explanation defining reporting relationships for each chairperson. Below are two sample job descriptions for chairpersons.

SAMPLE VOLUNTEER CHAIRPERSON JOB DESCRIPTIONS

1. Annual Fund Chairperson

The position of chairperson of St. Mary's Annual Fund is a two-year commitment. The chair attends all development team meetings, which are held in the evening of the second Tuesday of September, November, January, March, May, and July. The chair also calls interim meetings of his or her subcommittee, as necessary. As chair, you can expect to be busiest September through November and during our follow-up period in March.

The chair reports to the development team and works closely with our development director. The chair is responsible for supervising the annual fund committee.

The duties of the annual fund chairperson include:

- Recruiting subcommittee volunteers and solicitors
- Scheduling meetings
- Helping to set campaign goals and formulating strategy with the development director and principal
- Writing with the principal a letter for the annual fund appeal
- Coordinating with the public relations/publicity committee to assure sufficient publicity and timely mailing of the appeal
- Helping to make personal-gift solicitation calls and identify new prospects
- Seeing that written records are kept of procedures, volunteers, and expenses by subcommittee coordinators
- Keeping the development director abreast of committee activity
- Knowing and abiding by school policies on banking, and reporting funds collected and expended
- Planning a recognition event for major contributors
- Recognizing annual fund volunteers
- Participating in the annual review and evaluation of the year's campaign

2. Public Relations Chairperson

The position of chairperson of St. Mary's Public Relations Committee is a two-year commitment. The chair attends all development team meetings, which are held in the evening of the second Tuesday of September, November, January, March, May, and July. The chair also calls interim meetings of his or her committee, as necessary. Public relations is a year-round effort, so the chairperson can expect to be busy five to six hours a week most of the school year.

The chair reports to the development team and works closely with our development director.

The duties of the public relations/publicity chairperson include:

- Recruiting subcommittee volunteers and solicitors
- Scheduling meetings
- Helping to set goals and formulating strategy with the development director and principal
- Acting as liaison to the media, writing or editing press releases, and acting as spokesperson
- Creating and maintaining an up-to-date media list
- Creating and maintaining an up-to-date list of community, business, religious, educational, and political persons of influence who should be made aware of the school's activities

---

- Helping to survey and making suggestions regarding the school's image
- Coordinating with committee chairs to provide appropriate coverage of development activities
- Seeing that written records are kept of procedures, volunteers, and expenses by subcommittee coordinators
- Keeping the development director abreast of committee activity
- Knowing and abiding by school policies on banking, and reporting funds collected and expended
- Recognizing committee volunteers
- Participating in the annual review and evaluation of the year's program

Other items that should be included in the volunteer handbook are a profile sheet of the school, the school's mission and philosophy, and names and phone numbers of relevant staff and other volunteers. Policies regarding the use of school staff, equipment, and facilities provide guidelines for the volunteers and prevent problems from arising. Include a list of detailed procedures regarding how funds are collected, handled, banked, and disbursed. Add a projected calendar of development activities for the forthcoming year and lists of references and resource materials available to the volunteer. Put in anything at all that is relevant, such as a copy of the three- to five-year development plan and any long-range plans for the school. The final item to include is a reporting card for the volunteer to complete; see Worksheet 4.3 at the end of this chapter for a sample.

6. How do you support your volunteers?

Once you have recruited your volunteers, you inherit a responsibility to support them and see them through difficult times. First of all, pre-service your volunteers thoroughly on the mission and philosophy of your school and on exactly where they fit in. Provide ongoing inservice and opportunities for further training.

Set goals carefully by evaluating your chances for success, given what is reasonable and the resources available. Share your plans and goals with your volunteers first, and listen to their ideas. You have recruited these people for their expertise; let their input make a difference. Accepting another person's ideas is a high form of praise and may result in a better way of doing things.

Treat volunteers professionally. Review their work with them regularly, and keep accurate records of their contribution. See to it that volunteers have the resources they need to do the job. They may need such things as space in your school, access to copy machines, or a place to get coffee. Although these are very small items, providing them shows that you value your volunteers.

There are several ways of collecting volunteer-service information. You can have a volunteer send in the information on a monthly, quarterly, or project-by-project basis. Another method is to assign subcommittee chairs to collect the information at the completion of each project.

No matter what they say or how much they protest, everyone likes recognition for their efforts. Recognizing your volunteers' contribution to your school is the first step in reenlisting their services. Recognition need not be fancy, but it must be consistent. Minimum recognition should include a handwritten thank-you letter and mention in the annual report or special edition of the newsletter focusing on volunteers.

Build your program to include once-a-year celebration of volunteers either during Catholic Schools Week or National Volunteer Month (April) or at a summer year-end party. Have a ceremony and recognize anniversaries (2 years, 5 years, 10 years) and service hours (100 hours, 500 hours) and new recruits. Provide each volunteer with a certificate of appreciation.

7. What are some challenges in working with volunteers?

Working with volunteers presents special challenges. Volunteer managers lack the incentives that paid employees have, such as raises, bonuses, and promotions. Creativity is needed to provide incentives for volunteers and to meet the special challenges a volunteer program presents. Below are some common challenges with suggestions on how to meet them.

Turnover - To prevent the too-rapid turnover of volunteers, be sure they are well matched with their jobs and set terms of office for them. Set reasonable goals and ensure that the volunteers have the necessary resources for their job. Recognize volunteers for their efforts and celebrate their achievements.

Burnout - Know the signs: Your best volunteer shows little enthusiasm, misses meetings, does a poor job, sounds bitter about his or her task. Immediately offer some special recognition, such as a card or phone call. Set limits to volunteer terms, so the person doesn't feel committed to a life sentence. Offer volunteers opportunities to expand their potential, such as seminars, a chance to network with volunteers from other schools, workshops, classes. Promptly reimburse volunteers for any out-of-pocket expenses. Set time limits for meetings and keep to the schedule.

Low Priority - Set annual schedules early to allow volunteers easier personal planning. Adopt a professional stance, set deadlines, and expect that they will be met. Follow up on absences and missed deadlines. Let volunteers be among the first to hear school news, and let them know they are important by keeping them abreast of what's new. Be sure to link a specific volunteer name with a specific responsibility.

EDITOR'S NOTE: NCEA offers to schools in the fall the annual edition of its Catholic school volunteer Christmas ornament. This inexpensive ornament carries a special message for the volunteer.

(Carol Mack is owner of Carol Mack: Development Planning for the small nonprofit organization, Winsted, Connecticut, and is an associate of the Center for Institutional Advancement. She specializes in communication and volunteer organizations.)

Additional Reading on the Topic from NCEA

Shaughnessy, Mary Angela, Shaughnessy, John, and Coughlin, Maureen. (1993). *Volunteers in Catholic Schools: An Administrator's Guide to Legal Considerations.*

Tedesco, Janis. (1991). *Catholic Schools and Volunteers: A Planned Involvement.*

WORKSHEET 4.1

Volunteer Record Card

Volunteer Record Card
Thank you for giving the gift of time to our school!

Last Name_____First Name_____Middle Initial____

Preferred Form of Address (Please circle): Mr. Mrs. Ms. Miss Dr. Rev. Other_____

Home Address_____

City_____ State_____ Zip_____

Home Phone_____ Fax_____ Birthday_____

Business Address_____

City_____ State_____ Zip_____

Business Phone_____ Fax_____ Send Mail To ___Home ___Business

Spouse's Name_____

I am an alumnus/alumna, class of_____. My spouse is an alumnus/alumna, class of_____.

My children's names   Alumnus/alumna or current class year

_____   _____

_____   _____

_____   _____

I am willing to share the following skills, talents, or expertise:
_____

I am particularly interested in helping our school in the following way:
_____

I am affiliated with the following organizations in the community:
_____

Volunteer service began (date)_____

Job	Date Started	Ended	Approximate Hours
_____	_____	_____	_____
_____	_____	_____	_____
_____	_____	_____	_____

Special Achievements:_____
_____

Notes:_____
_____
_____

WORKSHEET 4.2

List of Volunteers for the Year

1. ANNUAL FUND

CHAIRPERSON_____

COORDINATORS:

Personal Solicitation _____

     Subcommittee Members:

         _____

         _____

         _____

         _____

Direct Mail _____

Phonathon _____

     Phonathon Callers:

         _____

         _____

         _____

         _____

         _____

Kickoff _____

Other _____

_____

2. PUBLIC RELATIONS/PUBLICITY

CHAIRPERSON _____

COORDINATORS:

Grandparents Day _____

Newsletter _____

Photography/Video _____

Historian _____

Mail _____

Other _____

_____

3. RECRUITMENT/RETENTION

CHAIRPERSON _____

COORDINATORS:

Preschool _____

Parish Baby Program_____

Open House_____

Other_____

4. SPECIAL EVENTS

EVENT_____

COORDINATOR:_____
  Subcommittee Members:

  _____
  _____
  _____

EVENT_____

COORDINATOR:_____
  Subcommittee Members:

  _____
  _____
  _____

EVENT_____

COORDINATOR:_____
  Subcommittee Members:

  _____
  _____
  _____

5. ALUMNI RELATIONS

CHAIRPERSON _____

Class Agents:

_____

_____

_____

_____

_____

Class Reunion Coordinators:

_____

_____

_____

_____

_____

NON-COMMITTEE VOLUNTEERS

JOB	VOLUNTEER

WORKSHEET 4.3

Reporting Card of Volunteer Services

Reporting Card of Volunteer Services

[School Logo]

Thank you for giving our school the gift of your time!
Please take a minute to fill out and return this card.

Volunteer Name_____

Project _____

Number of hours donated _____

Please complete and return this card by _____.

Send after a project is completed. Put your school name and address on the reverse side for convenient mailing back to the school.

Note: Perforated postcards to run through your copier or laser printer are available through several paper-supply catalogs and office-supply stores. Using these postcards is a convenient, inexpensive alternative to having them printed professionally.

CHAPTER 5:
PUBLIC RELATIONS/ MARKETING

Raymond L. John

This chapter will answer these questions:

1. What is meant by public relations/marketing on the elementary school level?
2. What are the benefits of doing this work?
3. What are the goals of public relations/marketing?
4. The school brochure is a tool for public relations/marketing. What information should be included in a school brochure?

1. What is meant by public relations/marketing on the elementary school level?

Public relations/marketing—the very title makes most of us in Catholic education a little nervous. Thoughts of crass commercialization come to mind. But, let's hold on for a minute. If by public relations and marketing we mean telling our story, well, why not? Catholic schools have been highly successful for hundreds of years. The public has a need and a right to hear our story. It is only when we tell our story that we can meet new people and give them an opportunity to share our success.

2. What are the benefits of doing this work?

Public relations is a wonderful way to add to your school's enrollment, gain support in the parish and community, and give others an opportunity to share in your school's success. Efforts to highlight your school's successes in the media will reap donations, grants, and endowments and ultimately help to ensure your school's future.

3. What are the goals of public relations/marketing?

Basically, there are five goals for public relations/marketing, as follows:
* To develop a community-wide public relations program for the school
* To gain access to larger media
* To work with community leadership
* To arrange special events to highlight the school in the community
* To develop a concise yet informative brochure

Goal 1: To develop a community-wide public relations program for the school. The important point is that the entire community needs to become aware of all that is going on at the school. The people in the community will come to expect to see school news and activities in the print and various other media. This is not hard to do, but it takes planning, preparation, and commitment. See Worksheet 5.1 for ideas on how to start.

Goal 2: To gain access to larger media. Local newspapers and local radio are tough enough to get into. The next group to strive for is the larger media (e.g., national print, television, Internet). The trick here is have a "hook." Television reporters will not cover a school event that is not exciting or eye-catching. Nobody is going to be on the six o'clock evening news for receiving first place in the school science fair.

The hook is that special story that intrigues the reporter or news desk. For example, St. Joseph's Elementary School has been on national TV, Bay Area TV, and in large metropolitan newspapers for its annual 49er Super Bowl Tailgate Party. Whether the 49ers win or lose the season, the school throws a huge outdoor tailgate party and rally for the children. Hot dogs are served, and the children and faculty dress up in the 49er red and gold colors. The school has a huge rally with sometimes as many as 700 to 800 people in attendance.

The advantage? Every time the tailgate party is aired, the reporter talks about the "fun at St. Joseph's Elementary School." Many people who come to register say their first knowledge of the school was through the television story. Worksheet 5.2 at the end of this chapter shows how to start the process.

Goal 3: To work with community leadership. Public relations is more than getting in the papers and on television. It is telling your story to all the people in the community so they can become a significant part of your school's present and future. This can be simple. Get to know the key players in the community. Make sure to meet and have a dialogue with the mayor, city council, public school superintendent, police and fire chiefs, leaders of service clubs, and other community leaders.

The advantages are infinite. Several years ago, I made solid contacts with the mayor of a small city. After two years of ongoing friendship, the mayor included our school in a community grant that netted over $150,000 in building upgrades for our school. See Worksheet 5.3 at the end of this chapter for ideas on working with community leadership.

Goal 4: To arrange special events to highlight the school in the community. Catholic school people do so many things so well that they tend to be a little humble. If you're going to tell your story, you need to toot your horn a little bit. Plan special events that can include the community. A Grandparents and Senior Citizens Day, for instance, would be really beneficial for the children and the community as well. A service requirement of hours of helping the community can be a reward for the students and the recipients. Just adding the words "community celebration" to the name of your annual events can be a big draw. See Worksheet 5.4 at the end of this chapter for this area of development.

Goal 5: To develop a concise yet informative brochure. Most people who come to a new community want to know how successful the schools are. It is important that you have a brochure that quickly yet thoroughly tells the school's story. Worksheet 5.5 at the end of this chapter will guide the planner through the production of a school brochure.

4. The school brochure is a tool for public relations/marketing. What information should be included in a school brochure?

The basic components of a brochure include information regarding the staff, religion program, academics, sports, families, and admission policy. Make brochures available to the parish office, local realtor, community leaders, etc.

Summary

Public relations/marketing is an extremely important component of any administrator's responsibilities. If work is done carefully on the five goals for public relations/marketing, the benefits will soon be reaped. There will be an increase in enrollment, donations, and volunteers and generally real acceptance and support from the entire parish community. Plan a good calendar that includes the five goals of public relations/marketing and you will find yourself regularly in the media.

(Raymond L. John, Ed.D., was principal of St. Joseph Elementary School in Alameda, California, at the time of this writing. He is now principal of Bishop Quinn High School and St. Francis Middle School in Palo Cedro, California.)

Additional Reading on the Topic from NCEA

Donaldson, Frank. (1991). *Catholic School Publications: Unifying the Image.*

WORKSHEET 5.1

Develop a Public Relations Campaign

School _____ Date_____

1.   Whom do I want to tell? (Community at large, parish, city, local neighbor)
      _____
      _____
      _____

2.   What is taking place? (Event, award, recognition ceremony)
      _____
      _____
      _____

3.   Why is it important? (School anniversary, significant for the community, service to others)
      _____
      _____
      _____

4.   Where, when, and how? (Exact location, date, and time; contact person)
      _____
      _____
      _____

5.   Whom do I want to contact? (Local editor, news desk, community bulletin board, cable TV community access)
      _____
      _____
      _____

6.   Evaluation (Coverage received, what went wrong, what went right)
      _____
      _____
      _____
      _____
      _____

After completing the six questions on this worksheet, the reader will be better able to successfully start a public relations campaign for his or her school.

WORKSHEET 5.2

Gain Access to Larger Media

1. Whom do I want to access? (Local TV, newspaper, CNN)

_____

_____

_____

_____

_____

2. What is the "hook"? What will pique the news desk editor?

_____

_____

_____

_____

_____

3. What is the best time to throw the hook? (It is better to have a Super Bowl tailgate party two weeks before the Super Bowl, before Super Bowl news is on practically all day and night.)

_____

_____

_____

_____

_____

4. Whom do I want to contact? (Names of local news editors, anchorpersons, etc.)

_____

_____

_____

_____

_____

5. Evaluation

_____

_____

_____

_____

_____

_____

_____

WORKSHEET 5.3

Work with Community Leadership

1. Who? (List your community leaders)

    _____
    _____
    _____
    _____
    _____

2. When? (Calendar these people as soon as possible)

    _____
    _____
    _____
    _____
    _____

3. What? (List the information about your school that you are trying to input)

    _____
    _____
    _____
    _____
    _____
    _____

4. Evaluation (Assess how the relationships have been beneficial to your school)

    _____
    _____
    _____
    _____
    _____
    _____

WORKSHEET 5.4

Arrange Special Events to Highlight the School in the Community

1.   What special event? (What can you do for the community?)

_____
_____
_____
_____

2.   When? (When will the event be held?)

_____
_____
_____
_____

3.   Effect on the school? (How will this event help the school?)

_____
_____
_____
_____

4.   Effect on the community? (How will this event help the community?)

_____
_____
_____
_____

5.   Evaluation (Were the effects of #3 and #4 worth the time and efforts?)

_____
_____
_____
_____

WORKSHEET 5.5

Develop a School Brochure

1. What do I need to say? (Be concise, yet thorough.)

    _____
    _____
    _____
    _____

2. What kind of "hook" do I need? (Color photography, great kid pictures, school symbol, etc.)

    _____
    _____
    _____
    _____

3. Who is going to produce it? (Hint: It's worth the money—always go professionally.)

    _____
    _____
    _____
    _____

4. Distribution (Who gets the brochure? In addition to parish and community leaders and members, distribute to new residents in the school community.)

    _____
    _____
    _____
    _____

5. Evaluation (List what needs to be replaced, re-edited, or changed to better demonstrate your school's excellence when the brochure is reprinted.)

    _____
    _____
    _____
    _____
    _____
    _____

CHAPTER 6:
RECRUITMENT AND RETENTION OF STUDENTS

Lorraine A. Hurley

This chapter will answer these questions:

1. What is recruitment and what are its goals and objectives?
2. What is short-range recruitment?
3. What is long-range recruitment?
4. What are the initial steps to increase enrollment?
5. What are the main sources for seeking out potential students?
6. What are some steps to take to involve the community in an effort to increase enrollment?
7. What are some preparatory steps to take to achieve the increase?
8. What kinds of communications are needed to achieve this goal?

1.   What is recruitment and what are its goals and objectives?

Recruitment is the process of actively seeking students to become members of the school community. The goals of recruitment are twofold: (a) short-range—to fill vacancies now, immediately for the upcoming academic year and (b) long-range—to meet future needs, assess the building's potential, determine classroom requirements, and retain waiting lists. The objectives of recruitment are to seek out potential students through several sources: from the parish community, the school community, and the municipal community.

2.   What is short-range recruitment?

Short-range recruitment is a coordinated effort to enroll enough students to fill your school for the upcoming academic year. To begin this process, it is important to assess your present needs. I suggest a checklist as an appropriate indicator. First, list the number of students currently in your school. Then assess the maximum number of students you can accept. This should be done for each grade level. Be specific.

	Current Number of Students in School	Maximum Number of Students to Accept	Number of Students to Recruit
	A	**B**	**(B less A)**
Preschool	_____	_____	_____
Kindergarten	_____	_____	_____
Grade 1	_____	_____	_____
Grade 2	_____	_____	_____
Grade 3	_____	_____	_____
Grade 4	_____	_____	_____
Grade 5	_____	_____	_____
Grade 6	_____	_____	_____
Grade 7	_____	_____	_____
Grade 8	_____	_____	_____
Totals	_____	_____	_____

It is important to make these numbers available to the school secretary, who will be the most likely person to receive inquiries via the phone.

3. What is long-range recruitment?

Long-range recruitment is a coordinated effort to assure the longevity of the school. It is essential that an approved plan of action be incorporated into the school's long-range plan. This can encompass a three- to five-year strategic growth and development plan. The topics that need to be seriously addressed might include (a) assessing the physical building potential: What is the school's capacity? Is there sufficient room capability, e.g., library space? (b) determining classroom requirements: What are the classroom requirements if we remain an elementary school? a middle school? a regional school? Can a program for 3- and 4-year-olds be incorporated? Will a second first grade, a second second grade, etc., be required? and (c) retaining waiting lists: Will waiting lists provide the stability that is required? Who is responsible for screening new applicants? Who maintains the files and communicates with these students and their families?

In a long-range plan for recruitment, it is extremely important to retain a list of future students. The main reason that such a list can become "lost in the shuffle" is failure to clearly define to whom this task is assigned. I suggest that a definite assignment be given to someone, either on staff or a volunteer, to track and communicate with these potential school families periodically. It will be time well invested.

4. What are the initial steps to increase enrollment?

To secure students for future needs, there needs to be in place an application process, a potential students file, and contact through mail or by phone. The principal or development personnel charged with finding recruits for the school needs to try a variety of means of communication. The best means, of course, is direct contact with potential students, without forgetting the power of the media and community involvement as sources of recruitment.

(a) **Where do I begin?**

Use past applications of students who were no-shows. Make a personal phone call and say, for example:

- "We have two unexpected vacancies in our second grade. Are you still interested?
- Can we hold a spot for you this fall?
- Is it possible that you may have further questions regarding our school's curriculum?
- Can I or someone else help or answer them for you?
- Would you like to stop by and tour our school again before the fall arrives?"

These are questions that can be used for seeking out students during the summer months, when you find unexpected openings in various grades. The *phone call* is the most effective way of reaching the undecided.

(b) **What type of person does recruitment best?**

The art of recruitment is manifested through the person who is actively involved in seeking students for a specific school and who possesses an honest, cheerful, and caring attitude toward each individual who is interviewed or contacted. The assignment of a recruiter for a school might be given to the development officer, if a school is fortunate enough to have one, or to a dedicated volunteer or to the school secretary. Actually, the principal and every faculty member are recruiters for the school in the very act of relating with parents and students.

5. What are the main sources for seeking out potential students?

The following three sources are the main areas upon which a school should focus:

(a) **The pastor** is a primary source, for he can give you a list of all the newly baptized. Such children are potential candidates for your parish school. Send a congratulatory card to the family. The pastor can also give you an update on newly arrived parishioners with children in the family. Send a welcome card to each family and an invitation to an open house. You can arrange with the pastor for bulletin board space in the church: Tell the good news about the school and highlight events to which potential students and their families are invited, e.g., activities for Catholic Schools Week.

Seek out the pastor for files on families in the parish who are sending their children to public schools. The pastor can grant you space in the weekly church bulletin so you can insert school news, especially vacancies or waiting lists for each classroom. Insert in the bulletin a survey that asks simple questions related to the school and recruitment of parish school-age children. Sample questions include, How long have you been a parishioner? Did you attend the parish school? If so, for how many years? Do you have school-age children? What are their ages and grade levels? Have you considered the parish school? If so, is your child enrolled here now? If not, what are your concerns? Would you encourage others to attend the parish school? The most important point is to direct your questions in a way that touches the parish consideration with a personal touch.

Thank the pastor and parishioners for this input and *use* the information to improve your recruitment techniques and to foster improved parish-community relations.

(b) **The principal** is a second source of information for recruiters for a parish school. Contact the principal as a resource for statistics. Use these data by incorporating them into recruitment efforts for present and future needs. Ask the principal for a schedule of events and activities. Invite, invite, invite potential students whenever possible: to spelling bees, basketball games, graduation, school picnics. Each month should offer an opportunity for future students to visit. Always request a student to escort a potential student through the building. One-on-one is your best means of contact.

(c) **The municipal community** can be a good source of recruitment potential. Become personally known by local-government educational officials so that they are aware of the quality education given at your school. Invite these government officials to visit on special occasions, e.g., Catholic Schools Week, National Library Week, or Reading Day. Ask government officials to speak on units of study such as elections, the town charter, government day, etc. Municipal services usually include giving tours. Plan field trips to take advantage of these tours: the local bank, police station, firehouse, bakery, etc. Conduct a real-estate day and invite agents to tour the school and ask questions. Exchange brochures.

6. What are some steps to take to involve the community in an effort to increase enrollment?

The key element is creativity. Find a reason for visitors to come, and make certain they will view something new and different. They may know many of the parents and students as well. Introduce them. Photograph the visitors. Thank the visitors for coming and ask them to come again. A telephone thank-you does not suffice; follow up with a sincerely written note.

Consider the following actual project: At St. Francis School in Naugatuck, Connecticut, an invitation to visit during Catholic Schools Week was sent out with a special request to attend a class and teach a subject or answer students' questions. Senators, representatives, and elected officials came. Each asked for a specific grade; for example, one of the representatives discussed the safety of wearing motorcycle helmets with the fourth grade. The fourth graders in turn wrote a law for the representative to incorporate into his planning. The official who visited the third grade discussed what she did when she was in the third grade. She stressed the value of study and homework. It turned out to be an unforgettable experience.

7. What are some preparatory steps to take to achieve the increase?

To secure the entrance of students for future years, examine your application process. Even though the application process seems clerical and bland, it is essential that it be well thought-out and well organized. The staff, who will be directly involved with the initial contact of the student and parent, should be well versed in the proper procedure of filling out the forms. Certainly, a hands-on workshop is important, with unexpected hypothetical questions asked so that the interviewer is well prepared.

It is helpful to color-code the forms; e.g., use blue for preschool, pink for kindergarten, yellow for grades one to five. Forms can also be numbered or lettered so that the proper person receives them: Use *N*, for instance, for those that should be given to the nurse. To portray a school where education is foremost, the process should be professional and efficient, including double-checking of spelling and grammar; making clear, clean copies of forms; and so forth.

Date and sign the registration form when received. This date will become important when you start waiting lists. Acknowledge receipt of forms personally when given or through the mail or via telephone.

Make sure the information form also requests facts that will become useful later. A sample question is, Did any member of your family attend this school? If yes, who_____ and when_____ (dates)? This specific information will become a needed resource when compiling alumni lists for a future alumni day.

Do not discard applications of those who applied but did not attend. As indicated earlier, such students may fill your short-range goals if there is an unexpected vacancy in a specific class.

Potential Students File - It is well established that statistics weigh heavily during the decision-making process of an adult. Since it is the parents' or legal guardians' choice as to where to send their child/children, you would be wise to make notes regarding each child. The factors that may affect the adults' decision can vary. Following are certain common concerns: How many students will be in the class? How many of the child's friends are coming? Will friends travel on the same bus? Will brothers and sisters also be on the same bus? What time will the child be picked up and dropped off? Does the school have after-school day-care services? If so, until what hour?

The list of questions is endless, especially when uncertainty is involved. If the staff do not have an answer to a potential student's question, then seek out the answer with facts to support it, note it, and convey it to the parents. It may be an answer that will assist them in choosing your school for their child.

Contact Through Mail or by Phone - Correspondence with potential students and their families is most effective if the following steps are taken: (a) Answer requests promptly. (b) Address the parents or legal guardians appropriately by name, as opposed to using a form response. (c) Date all correspondence. (d) Indicate when the school office is open so forms can be dropped off or when visits are possible. (e) Invite them to call if they have questions.

Telephone requests for information regarding the school, the application process, tuition, etc., should be answered promptly and in a courteous manner. Be sensitive to the fact that the caller may detect that the timing is not appropriate. Caution the office personnel to call back and speak further about admissions. Request a phone number and a time when the caller can be reached. At all times, proper telephone etiquette should prevail. If we took the extra trouble to be kind and helpful to inquiring parents so that each phone call enrolled one student, our schools would be overflowing.

8. What kinds of communications are needed to achieve this goal?

Utilize a Variety of Means of Communication - The personal approach—the eye-to-eye or, as it is commonly called, the one-to-one approach—is the most effective tool in recruitment. For example, at an open-house event, ask the visitors to sign in. Make an effort to memorize their names, especially since one visit may not be sufficient. Encourage questions. Arrange for tours of the entire school. Display books, curricula, and especially *the students' work.* Allow visitors to sit in a classroom and to talk to the teachers, staff, and other parents. Introduce visitors to everyone within view and, above all, thank them for coming. During Catholic Schools Week, provide daily opportunities for potential students and their families to visit, and include all the above means of welcoming visitors to the school.

Media - The newspaper is the prime media source for an entire community. Become acquainted with a specific reporter. Keep him or her informed of recruitment events, such as open house and Catholic Schools Week. Publish facts such as alumni involvements. An approach that appeals to a reporter is to say, "Did you know that St. Francis School did this? Did you know that our graduates achieved high honors (or special recognition) in this high school?" Actively seek out high interest points for the local newspaper. Have the newspaper delivered to the school office; newspapers respect subscribers' opinions and input. Radio and television are fine sources for advertisements but, unfortunately, are expensive. When several schools, such as a region, collaborate in a unified ad, however, the results can be very positive. Many radio stations do offer free public service announcements, so take advantage of them.

Community Involvement - Since the majority of students will attend the school from within the community, it is strongly suggested to keep the community informed of all school happenings. The best means to achieve this objective centers on service projects to the community by the students. The list can be endless. Certain classes can visit nursing homes and hospitals. Invitations can be sent to the community for the school's Christmas pageant and spring concert. Students can write thank-you notes to the bus drivers, police officers, and fire department personnel. Allow the school building to be used by community groups, such as the Knights of Columbus and Little Leagues. Collect clothes and food for the homeless or for a family in time of tragedy. Certainly, the parents, students, teachers, and staff can suggest volunteer service projects that may be administered to the community. The fact that the values of a Catholic school are put into the community would certainly convince many parents to send their children to a school with Christian concern for their neighbor.

Summary

Recruitment is a very important phase of the development program, since without students, there can be no schools. The process is continuous and should not be relaxed during certain times of the year, such as the summer. Each season has a reason to recruit students. Be creative. Be energetic. Be involved. (Refer to Worksheets 6.1 and 6.2 at the end of the chapter for sample forms to use.) The best recruitment tool is a school with a strong program of studies that reflects a spirit of learning within the ideals and values of the Catholic faith.

This chapter on recruitment was prepared to be a basic beginning tool. The suggestions work and are workable. Need proof? In 1992-1993, St. Francis in Naugatuck, Connecticut, had a student enrollment of 243. After efforts that include all the ones listed in this chapter, in the 1995-1996 school year, St. Francis had a school enrollment of 320 with waiting lists!

This chapter also was specifically centered around the premise that students should be the main focus in fulfilling the mission and philosophy of a Catholic elementary school. The successful completion of their education is the barometer whereby a school can judge its competency. The parents/legal guardians who seek a Catholic school for their child are the scales upon which to weigh a perpetuating recruitment plan.

(Lorraine A. Hurley is principal of St. Francis of Assisi School in Naugatuck, Connecticut.)

Additional Reading on the Topic from NCEA

Monetti-Souply, Marta. (1990). *A Year-round Recruitment and Retention Plan.*

Dernovek, Mary. (1989). *Letters to Parents of Preschool Children.*

WORKSHEET 6.1

Student Recruitment Checklist

Goals for_____ in the
                     (School Name)

Academic Year_____

1.   SHORT-RANGE GOALS

_____
_____
_____

2.   LONG-RANGE GOALS

_____
_____
_____

Step 1 -   The present enrollment is_____
              (Identify the numbers in each class)

              The projected enrollment for_____is_____
                                  (year)
              (Identify the number of students to be recruited for each class.)

Step 2 -   To recruit, the following person will be the contact for the school:

              Name_____

              Phone_____

              Days Available_____

Step 3 -   The following means will be used:
                                          Date
              a.   Brochure   _____
              b.   Open House   _____
              c.   Mail   _____
              d.   Newspaper   _____
              e.   Radio/TV/E-Mail   _____

Step 4 -   The following individuals will comprise the committee:

_____
_____
_____

WORKSHEET 6.2

Student Recruitment Plan

A. STUDENT GOAL SETTING

Total Student Body Goal for [*Next Year*]:_____

	Pre-K	K	1	2	3	4	5	6	7	8
[*Next Year*]	____	____	____	____	____	____	____	____	____	____

Actual Student Population per Grade
(Students registered now for September [*Current Academic Year*])

[*Current Year*]	____	____	____	____	____	____	____	____	____	____

Projected Student Retention per Grade for [*Next Academic Year*]

____ ____ ____ ____ ____ ____ ____ ____ ____ ____

New Students to Be Recruited per Grade for [*Next Academic Year*]
(This is the goal for the student recruitment committee)

____ ____ ____ ____ ____ ____ ____ ____ ____ ____

B. SPECIAL STUDENT RECRUITMENT ACTIVITIES
(Planned within recommended calendar of student recruitment activities)

September

October

November

December

January

February

March

April [*Day, Year*] - Registrations Close for [*Next Academic Year*]

CHAPTER 7:
CASE STATEMENT

Raymond L. John

This chapter will answer these questions:
1. What is a case statement?
2. What are the necessary components of a case statement?
3. How do you formulate a case statement?
4. How is a case statement used?

1. What is a case statement?

A case statement is a customized document concerning your school that incorporates its mission, goals, and objectives and presents a comprehensive picture of the school. It is used when recruiting volunteers, requesting large donations and gifts from major donors, and seeking to enhance public awareness of your school.

2. What are the necessary components of a case statement?

A case statement includes a brief summary of the school's purpose, its history, its contributions to the community, plans for the future, and projected activities to accomplish these goals.

Generally, a school is ready to do a case statement if it has developed a philosophy, a mission statement, and a strategic plan and has a written history. Most of the above are usually accomplished at the time of a school site self-evaluation or of an external accreditation process.

3. How do you formulate a case statement?

The following work is prerequisite to developing a case statement:
* State your school philosophy.
* State your school's mission statement.
* Highlight your school's goals and objectives from your strategic plan.
* Give a four- to five-paragraph history of your institution.

If you have done all of the above, you are ready to put together a 10- to 15-page case statement to present to major donors. If you have not done each item above, you must complete them *before* you do the case statement.

If you have completed all of the items above, put them together in a simple format:
A. School's Purpose (Incorporate philosophy and mission statement)
B. History
C. School's Contributions to the Community
D. Plans for the Future (Include goals and objectives)
E. Plans to Accomplish These Goals
F. Investment Opportunities (Detail three areas: endowment, capital improvements, and arranged giving programs)

4. How is a case statement used?

A case statement can be used for at least three purposes:

(a) **Major donors** - A case statement is perfect for soliciting major donors and large granters.

List the donors in your area to whom you would consider sending a case statement. Also list the grants for which your school is eligible.

(b) **Public awareness** - A case statement is your best way to communicate your story in a detailed manner. It is much more than a short brochure with a few highlights. Anyone reading the case statement will really know who you are and where you are headed. Remember, every time someone outside of your school buys into your program, you have a friend, a possible contributor, and, ultimately, a benefactor. Use the who-what-why-how-when exercise in Worksheet 7.1 at the end of this chapter to determine how you will generate greater public awareness.

(c) **National recognition** - A case statement is a great tool for gaining local and national recognition. It may enhance an application for school recognition; judges realize that a school with an excellent case statement has done its homework.

You need to research the award opportunities that are available. For example, recently our school, St. Joseph Elementary, received the national Blue Ribbon Schools Program Award from the U.S. Department of Education. The judges were impressed with our ability to articulate our present and future plans through our case statement.

Summary

A case statement is the first step beyond "beginning development." As you complete the case statement, you become a member of the next step in development—the advanced group. If you follow the guidelines and samples in this chapter and take the time to fill in all the blanks in Worksheet 7.1, you will be well on your way to initiating an effective development program.

(Raymond L. John, Ed.D., was principal of St. Joseph Elementary School in Alameda, California, at the time of this writing. He is now principal of Bishop Quinn High School and St. Francis Middle School in Palo Cedro, California.)

WORKSHEET 7.1

Generating Public Awareness

1. Whom do you want to make aware of your school and its wonderful qualities?

    _____

    _____

    _____

2. What do you want to make them aware of?

    _____

    _____

    _____

3. Why should they be aware of this?

    _____

    _____

    _____

4. How can you accomplish this?

    _____

    _____

    _____

5. When will it be achieved?

    _____

    _____

    _____

CHAPTER 8:
ANNUAL GIVING

Raymond L. John

This chapter will answer these questions:
1. What is annual giving?
2. What are the five goals of an annual giving campaign?
3. What is the process for starting an annual giving campaign?
4. How do you conduct an annual giving campaign?

1. What is annual giving?

An annual giving campaign is a component of a total development program. It is an effort to get an annual contribution for the school from each person connected with the school community directly and anyone else who might be an admirer or supporter. Everyone is a potential donor. It is a later step in the development process, following the solid strategic plan, case statement, public relations program, etc.

An annual giving campaign is generally the last piece of the complete development program because it takes the longest to get off the ground. All the work done in development prior to the annual giving campaign ensures that the program will be successful. The worksheets at the end of this chapter will give you a blueprint for starting a good annual giving program.

2. What are the five goals of an annual giving campaign?

The five basic goals of an annual giving campagin are:
- To get 100 percent of the school board to participate
- To get 100 percent of the faculty and staff to participate
- To get 100 percent of the families to participate
- To get participation from alumni
- To get participation from benefactors in the community

Goal 1: To get 100 percent of the school board to participate. Each member of the school board should be involved in the annual giving program. If every member gives something, no matter what amount given, it shows solid support for the school. A simple statement that the school board is behind the drive has greater impact when all the members have given something.

Goal 2: To get 100 percent of the faculty and staff to participate. The argument to support this goal is the same as for Goal 1. Again, if the people who work in the school support it by their donation, it shows they also "walk the talk."

Goal 3: To get 100 percent of the school families to participate. By far, this is the toughest goal. Families are already making financial sacrifices to pay the tuition. Once they realize that what they are paying does not meet the true per-pupil cost, many will want to be involved. A further incentive is the tax-deductibility of their contribution.

This goal, admittedly, is a lofty one—generally 40 to 50 percent participation of the families is considered quite successful.

Goal 4: To get participation from alumni. Notice a percentage is not stated here. The reasons are simple and varied: It takes years and years of annual giving programs before the alumni start coming around. Sometimes they are waiting for a son or daughter to finish college before they have "extra" money for other things. The main point to remember is to keep including the alumni in all your mailings, invitations, and acknowledgments. Eventually, they will become the largest givers.

Goal 5: To get participation from benefactors in the community. Like Goal 4, this one takes years to fully develop. Again, continue to bring the community into the life of the school through mailings, invitations, and acknowledgments. Consider all good media press that you work to achieve a good step in getting your successes known. Eventually, several benefactors will start giving. That early group will be the ones that get other benefactors to give. Consider asking all the businesses that service the school for a contribution. Consider asking businesses in the parish that have had alumni work in their offices or plants through the years for a donation. Consider asking former faculty, principals, and pastors. Be creative. Everyone is a potential donor!

3. What is the process for starting an annual giving campaign?

First, form an annual giving committee. This group needs to consist of board members, faculty, parents, alumni, and benefactors—representatives named from each of the entities stated above. After reviewing the lists of candidates, decide on which people from those lists should be on the committee. (Hint: Avoid soliciting people who already serve on several committees because this group will spend a considerable amount of time in meetings.) A reasonable number would be 10-15 people. The committee needs to be chaired by either a board member or a designated staff member (preferably a development director, if you are fortunate enough to have one). Worksheet 8.1 at the end of this chapter provides a means to collect important data for members of the annual giving committee.

After the annual giving committee is formed, it needs to set a purpose for the monies collected this year. The donors want to know how the funds will be used. No one will give money "to help" the school when he or she doesn't know exactly for what the funds are to be used. Pick specific items that the school really needs: computer equipment, new desks, new rugs, sports equipment, etc. At the end of this chapter, Worksheet 8.2 will help you to focus on the particular needs of your school.

Thirdly, the committee needs to agree on the target goal: How much money will secure what is needed? Normally, there are two or three goals, such as sports equipment, science lab renovation, and professional development fund.

Finally, the annual giving committee needs to establish a timeline of activities to achieve its goals. The campaign should be finished within three months. Worksheet 8.3 at the end of this chapter will help you plan the annual giving campaign.

4. How do you conduct an annual giving campaign?

Your committee is in place. Your target goals are set. You know how much money you need to obtain the target goals. You are now ready to begin. The pieces described below need to be prepared; see Worksheet 8.4 at the end of this chapter for a sample checklist. If you have access to a printing company (an alumnus or parishioner who is willing to do gratis work for the school or parish), you are all set. If you must, use your own school or parish duplication system.

First, you need a touching, warm, and inviting appeal letter. The letter should make people want to give to the cause. State exactly how much is needed and the time frame within which you would like the donation. Some people like to be asked a particular amount.

You need lists of those to whom you will send the appeal. The school can furnish you with the families of the children in the school. The parish can give you the parishioners without children. Try not to send duplicate letters to the same people. Send the appeals beyond the school and parish community. Get names and addresses of businesses the school and parish use as well as big businesses located in the city that are very fond of donating locally if it means added business and some public acknowledgments of their gifts.

Envelopes and postage for the appeal letter are part of the preparations. Another must is a card to be filled out and returned with the donation and a return envelope already printed with the name and address of the committee member who is charged with receiving the donations. This person may very well be the pastor or the principal or the president of the school board. The return envelope need not have postage already on it. Many appeal letters contain the statements: "Thank you for using your own stamp. It is an added gift to this appeal."

Thank-you notes and acknowledgments are most essential parts of this annual giving section. A rule of thumb is, You can never thank a donor enough times. A telephone call plus a letter should be responses for unusual gifts. Gifts from businesses in the local area should be acknowledged publicly—in the press or parish bulletin.

Anyone who receives an appeal letter and comes up with an idea for soliciting more money to accomplish the goal should be encouraged to follow through. It might be to "chance off" a handmade afghan or hold a bake sale.

Posters in the school or church foyer and in parish centers serve as reminders that the appeal is in process. Indicators of how successful the campaign is, e.g., thermometers containing information of what the goal is and how close the actual response to the goal is, are also very effective. Creative thinking here can keep the appeal at full interest.

For assistance with your campaign wrap-up and evaluation, use Worksheets 8.5 and 8.6 at the end of the chapter.

(Raymond L. John, Ed.D., was principal of St. Joseph Elementary School in Alameda, California, at the time of this writing. He is now principal of Bishop Quinn High School and St. Francis Middle School in Palo Cedro, California.)

Additional Reading on the Topic from NCEA

Oldenburg, Rick L. (1991). *Conducting the Phonothon.*

Tracy, Mary. (1990). *Steps in Direct Solicitation: Preparation, Presentation, and Follow-up.*

WORKSHEET 8.1

Forming the Annual Giving Committee

School_____ Date _____

SUGGESTED CANDIDATES

School Board Members

_____
_____
_____
_____

Qualifications

_____
_____
_____
_____

Faculty and Staff

_____
_____
_____
_____

Qualifications

_____
_____
_____
_____

School Parents

_____
_____
_____
_____

Qualifications

_____
_____
_____
_____

Alumni

_____
_____
_____
_____

Qualifications

_____
_____
_____
_____

Benefactors

_____
_____
_____
_____

Qualifications

_____
_____
_____
_____

WORKSHEET 8.2

Determining the Needs of the School

List needs of the school, approximate costs, and priority.

PRIORITY	NEED	COST
_____	_____	_____
_____	_____	_____
_____	_____	_____
_____	_____	_____
_____	_____	_____
_____	_____	_____
_____	_____	_____
_____	_____	_____
_____	_____	_____
_____	_____	_____
_____	_____	_____
_____	_____	_____
_____	_____	_____
_____	_____	_____
_____	_____	_____
_____	_____	_____

WORKSHEET 8.3

Timeline for Planning the Annual Giving Campaign

Starting date for committee meetings: _____

Additional meeting dates: _____

_____

_____

_____

First letter for annual giving: _____

Follow-up letters: _____

_____

_____

_____

Follow-up phone calls: _____

_____

_____

_____

Target Goals:

Date	Amount	Desired Item
_____	_____	_____
_____	_____	_____
_____	_____	_____
_____	_____	_____
_____	_____	_____
_____	_____	_____
_____	_____	_____
_____	_____	_____
_____	_____	_____
_____	_____	_____

WORKSHEET 8.4

Checklist for Planning the Annual Giving Campaign

TASK	PERSON RESPONSIBLE
Appeal letter	
Mailing lists	
School families	
Parishioners	
Businesses used by parish/school	
Local businesses	
Corporations	
Envelopes and stamps	
Pledge cards/return envelopes	
Posters	
Barometers of response	

WORKSHEET 8.5

Checklist for the Annual Giving Campaign Wrap-up

	TASK	PERSON RESPONSIBLE
_____	Final tally	_____
_____	Donor thank-yous	_____
_____	Thank-you phone calls	_____
_____	Committee thank-yous	_____
_____	Purchase and "showcase" of needed items	_____
_____	Evaluation (See Worksheet 8.6)	_____
_____	Preplan for following year	_____
_____	Thank-you party	_____

WORKSHEET 8.6

Evaluation of Annual Giving Program

Best things that happened:

1. _____
2. _____
3. _____
4. _____

Worst things that happened:

1. _____
2. _____
3. _____
4. _____

What to repeat next year:

1. _____
2. _____
3. _____
4. _____

What to avoid next year:

1. _____
2. _____
3. _____
4. _____

CHAPTER 9:
ALUMNI PROGRAM

Bill MacNeill

This chapter will answer these questions:

1. Why involve the alumni in a school development program?
2. What is the goal of an alumni program?
3. What are the benefits of an alumni program?
4. What are the basic elements of an alumni program?
5. How do you begin the process of starting an alumni program?
6. What event might start off an alumni reunion?
7. What is a typical process for organizing a grand school and parish reunion?

1.   Why involve the alumni in a school development program?

The alumni are often overlooked in creating an elementary school development program. This is unfortunate, since the alumni are the group who benefitted most directly from the work of the school's faculty and staff. In many cases, they paid little or no tuition for their education.

The common belief that graduates would not be interested in their "grammar" school is inaccurate. The fact is former students have a strong attraction and sense of gratitude for their teachers and "their" school. Too often, however, alumni are not asked to become involved.

2.   What is the goal of an alumni program?

The overall goal of an effective alumni program is to establish a mutually beneficial relationship between the school and its graduates. A natural bond is already there; a sense of gratitude is already there. Gratitude breeds a desire to "give back" something precious one has received. We need to capitalize on that idea of giving back.

3.   What are the benefits of an alumni program?

The alumni program creates an effective structure that enables the school leadership to utilize a valuable school resource. Alumni can provide an important source of financial support. True, you must do some homework in order to identify prospects and cultivate them before you can solicit support. The alumni program is a great asset in this process.

An alumni program can create a pool of talent to assist the school as volunteers on boards and committees and assist with technical expertise. Every school needs contacts with businesses. The alumni program can provide a resource to reach out to businesses and other agencies. The mutual benefit the alumni can receive for all this giving is contact with their grammar school, which can still provide spiritual (by holding periodic days of recollection or providing speakers on spiritual topics); social (by sponsoring various holiday dinner/dances); and other services to them in keeping with the school's mission.

4. What are the basic elements of an alumni program?

Like all aspects of development, an alumni program should involve:

• **Careful Planning** - A successful program requires a long-term view but with a strategic plan for each year. It is an ongoing program. One school calls its alumni "lifelong friends," for surely they are an intricate part of a school's history.

• **Assignment of Responsibility** - Someone has to be in charge. Although volunteer support is essential, ideally, someone on the school staff or a strongly committed volunteer needs to make sure things happen in an effective way. The alumni "director" helps plan the alumni program with the principal; gathers and maintains alumni records (see Worksheet 9.1 at the end of this chapter); recruits, organizes, and supports committees that carry out alumni events and activities; prepares the alumni newsletter and other publications; and acts as liaison between the alumni and the school.

• **Continuity** - An effective alumni program is carried out on a continuing basis, each year building on the one before it. Stop-and-go efforts cause a loss of interest and duplication of effort.

• **A Budget and Office Resources** - Sufficient funds for postage, stationery, and other resources (space, office equipment) must be allocated to ensure success. This is a capital investment that will pay dividends later.

• **Commitment by School Leaders** - The pastor and principal have to give appropriate time and energy to the alumni program. It must be a top priority. Time must be given to "cultivate" prospects, to wine and dine them, if necessary, to win their support for the benefit of your school. A most effective cultivation method is to involve alumni in the work of the school by serving on committees and boards and working on projects.

5. How do you begin the process of starting an alumni program?

The following steps are basic to the creation of an effective alumni program:

• **Compile alumni lists** - These lists need not include only graduates. Many schools involve those who did not graduate but attended for a period of time. Often, present or former parishioners as well as past faculty and staff are included in mailings of invitations to events.

First, create a raw listing (names and original addresses) from school records and other sources, such as high school yearbooks in the diocese where past alumni have attended. In older schools, if there are no existing records it is probably prudent to start at the 50-year mark and work toward the present. Volunteers can do much of this gathering. This raw listing should be placed on a computer database that has software that allows for updating and easy retrieval of information.

• **Find current addresses and other information** - There are three general categories of alumni: active (on record), missing, and deceased. Although names and addresses are basic information, other data such as phone numbers, occupations, and job titles can be most helpful. There are many methods by which current information on alumni can be recovered. The following are a few possibilities; a little brainstorming will produce others.

(a) Establish a committee to aid in finding missing alumni. The committee should cover a span of years and/or geographical areas. An event such as a reunion provides focus for such an undertaking. In most instances, a large percentage of graduates remain in the area or state. Most schools have had several family members attend; find one and the rest will follow. Many present students have parents and other relatives who attended the school.

(b) Start an alumni newsletter. This is an effective vehicle for finding missing graduates and maintaining contact. Local papers will often print the names of missing alumni. Paid advertisements can be helpful. Public announcements of a reunion or other event will cause people to respond.

(c) Ask for information through parish bulletins in the area. One school had an alumni booth at a local fair. The annual phonathon is an excellent source of new addresses and missing alumni as well as pledges of financial support. Even telephone directories can be a source, particularly if the name is distinctive. Very often, parents or family still live at the original address.

(d) Purchase CD-ROM discs that contain addresses and other information at a reasonable cost. Some commercial firms will publish an alumni directory and undertake research if the school meets certain criteria.

6. What event might start off an alumni reunion?

An approach used by many elementary schools to create up-to-date alumni records while developing wonderful good will in the process is the grand school and parish reunion. This approach capitalizes on the nostalgia and good feelings present among the school's graduates and present and former parishioners. Although it requires considerable time and effort, the results have proven this approach to be most worthwhile.

7. What is a typical process for organizing a grand school and parish reunion?

Set a date approximately one year away for a grand parish and school reunion. If there is a significant anniversary (the school's or parish's 25th, 30th, 40th anniversary), make use of it. In a parish school situation, consider all present and past parishioners part of the celebration and, as such, invited guests to the celebration.

Under the guidance of the alumni director, establish a reunion committee of activists, seeking a representative span of years: someone to gather information about alumni from the classes of 1960 to 1965, etc.; someone to get current addresses for the alumni from 1966 to 1969, etc. They will expand the committee, find the missing, and in collaboration with the school leaders, plan the event or events. Give the committee the existing lists of graduates from the school's records. On almost every committee, individuals will appear whose sole mission in life seems to have been keeping track of everyone else! Treasure them.

During this year, leaders will emerge who will take over the grand parish and school reunion. They will plan the menu, decorate the hall, print and sell tickets, and do the myriad things necessary to produce a truly fine event. Plan to give an award to any outstanding workers who really contributed the most to bringing the grand reunion to a successful conclusion.

After the event, you should have a pretty accurate alumni list, together with updated addresses and other pertinent information. Keep these people connected to the school. Plan small events, as an evening of prayer, during significant seasons (Lent, Advent). Start an alumni publication featuring alumni from certain years: what they are doing, their families, their successes or awards. Mail at least twice a year requesting address corrections from the U.S. Postal Service, to keep alumni and friends lists current. Creative thinking will find ways to keep the alumni program vibrant and active after the grand parish and school reunion.

(Bill MacNeill retired after 35 years of service as vice president for development at Boston College High School in Dorchester, Massachusetts. He presently serves as director of development for the Diocese of Wheeling-Charleston, West Virginia, and is an associate of the Center for Institutional Advancement in New York.)

WORKSHEET 9.1

[*Your School's Name*] Alumni Survey

Date_____

1. Name _____ Class_____
   Address_____
   (Number, Street or Avenue)

   _____
   (City, State, Zip Code)

2. Marital Status (Circle one):
   Married   Single   Widower   Divorced   Remarried
   If a married alumna, please give your maiden name:_____

3. Wife's or Husband's Full Name, if not an alumnus:

   _____
   Did spouse attend [*Your School's Name*]?   Yes_____   No_____
   Graduated?   Yes_____   Year_____   No _____

4. Years You Attended [*Your School's Name*]:   From_____ To_____
   Graduated?   Yes_____ No _____
   If a nongraduate, please list school(s) attended and year you graduated from elementary
   school:
   _____ From_____ To_____
   _____ From_____ To_____ Graduated _____
   (Year)

5. High School Attended: _____
   From _____ To _____   Year Graduated _____

6. Colleges and/or Universities Attended; Degree, Year, Major (Include undergraduate,
   graduate, and professional schools, even if degrees were not earned):

   _____
   _____
   _____
   Academic Honors (What and where?):_____
   _____

7. Children (Names and birthdates): _____
   _____
   _____

8. Relatives Who Have Attended [*Your School's Name*] (Please indicate relationship to you,
   the class, and current address):

   _____
   _____
   _____

CHAPTER 10:
EDUCATIONAL ENDOWMENT

Gary G. Wilmer

This chapter will answer these questions:

1. What are the usual sources of the elementary school's income, and how can they be changed?
2. What is an educational endowment?
3. Why is an educational endowment fund necessary?
4. What is a sample process to use to establish an educational endowment?
5. Which personnel should be directly involved in establishing the endowment?
6. What questions should be asked if a school wants to establish an educational endowment fund?
7. How do you start the process of establishing an educational endowment?
8. What results can a school expect in the first year's efforts?

1. What are the usual sources of the elementary school's income, and how can they be changed?

At present, many Catholic elementary schools and some secondary schools find themselves dependent on two sources of income. The first source includes tuition, fees, and, in some cases, limited school fund-raising. The second source is a direct subsidy from general parish (or small cluster of parishes) revenues. A positive plan of action to ensure the continuation of quality Catholic education could be an endowment fund. This could result in holding down major increases in tuition and parish subsidy to the school. With an endowment in place, the affordability of Catholic education can be maintained as a result of a plan developed from a position of strength.

2. What is an educational endowment?

An endowment fund is monies or securities that are set aside in a trust account or bank account. Only the earnings (or interest) on these invested funds should be used in the day-to-day operations of the school. An educational endowment is an attractive third source of income because an endowment can continue forever. It can provide a steady source of school income that can be relied on year after year. An endowment provides an ongoing investment-challenge opportunity for the entire parish or cluster of parishes. A well-managed endowment frequently attracts large gifts or bequests from within and outside the community. Please remember the strength of an endowment is that capital funds remain intact and the annual yield may provide a third source of income to complement other sources of income.

3. Why is an educational endowment fund necessary?

First of all, parishioners need to be made aware that even if they do not have children in the local parish school, in financially supporting it, they are doing what Jesus asked—to teach all nations. Evangelization of the parish's own children should be a primary concern. The values inculcated in the daily life of the children in a parish school are well worth the investment in their future. At the same time, parishioners need to be made aware of the rising cost of tuition and the fact that already many families cannot afford to educate their children in a Catholic school, much as they may want to. Tuition needs to be made affordable and kept stable. Escalating tuition will surely cause the demise of a school. Parishes for years have been contributing to the running of the parish school, but even a parish can use only so much of its resources to subsidize the parish school. By learning these few facts, parishioners can see the great need for the concept of a third source of income.

What follows is the process we used to plan for the future of St. Charles Elementary School in Minneapolis, Minnesota, a process we shared with the total parish community and larger school community. In 1989, we reflected on the following year's third-grade class. That year, the next fall's third-grade class would be the high school graduating class in the year 2000. That class and those who would follow must continue to be trained mentally and spiritually to be the caring and productive leaders of tomorrow. We proposed a positive plan of action to ensure quality education for our children while holding down major increases in tuition and parish subsidy in the future. In this way, the affordability of Catholic education would be maintained as a result of a plan developed from a position of strength.

At that time, our parish school maintained its day-to-day operations from two sources of income: (a) tuition, fees, and limited school fund-raising and (b) a direct subsidy from general parish revenues. Without question, it was clear that another source of income must be developed to strengthen the future of Catholic education in our thriving school. This third source of income would provide annual and predictable revenue to offset the rising costs of tuition and the parish subsidy. We proposed the establishment of the St. Charles Borromeo Catholic Education Endowment.

4. What is a sample process to use to establish an educational endowment?

The process we used at St. Charles Elementary School involved two phases. The first phase of the endowment was funded with a minimum investment of $1,000,000 that was raised through a major parish-wide capital fund-raising campaign that commenced early in the school year and continued throughout the fall. Every parishioner was invited to participate both financially and voluntarily. The campaign invited pledge commitments one year, with payment of the pledges over a 36-month period. Following the three-year pledge-payout period, the fund reached $1,000,000 in resources, yielding approximately $100,000 annually in interest and dividends. This was the minimum amount needed to attain the immediate goal of creating the third source of reliable and very stable income for the school community.

The second phase of the endowment was a long-term plan, focused well into the first decade of the 21st century, with an eye toward raising an additional $3,000,000 in commitments, which would bring the total return for school operational support to $400,000 annually. These funds would be raised through planned-gift opportunities, including, but not limited to, a bequest provision in wills, life insurance agreements, a charitable annuity, a charitable trust, and other avenues of deferred giving. Phase II commitments would be invited at the same time that Phase I gifts would be solicited.

5. Which personnel should be directly involved in establishing the endowment?

Essential to the success of the program at St. Charles Elementary School was an advisory committee comprised of members of the community with expertise and credentials in the financial community. They consulted with the parish leadership and others concerning the investment and management of endowment funds in order to ensure maximum safe growth, as wise stewards of these resources. Appropriate legal documents and agreements were set up to govern all gifts. The key to the management and operation of the endowment will be the creation of a trust agreement or "instrument" as a guideline for managing the fund. This instrument will be a legal document with provisions built in to protect the school and parish from any potential alteration or movement of funds contrary to the expressed purpose of funding the operation of the parish school.

The parish must seek competent and professional assistance in the management of the endowment. There are a number of highly qualified men and women from the parish with outstanding expertise in the financial community. These people will be assembled to provide counsel to the pastor and finance committee in order to ensure the maximum and safe growth of the fund.

As the endowment grows on a yearly basis, the school will be able to depend on the annual yield that such an endowment can produce. In this model of funding, the assets will remain untouched, managed carefully and responsibly by a qualified committee of investment advisors, and the interest will be used to support the school.

An essential component is to share as much information as possible with the school and parish community, those who made gifts to the fund. See below for a sample agenda of the steering committee meeting.

SAMPLE AGENDA FOR MEETING OF THE STEERING COMMITTEE

[Date, Time, and Place]

1.	Opening prayer and welcome	Chairperson
2.	Review A. Where we have been B. Where we are now C. Where we are going	Chairperson
3.	Presentation of video	Chairperson
4.	Review of campaign organization materials A. Campaign organization B. Campaign calendar C. Theme D. Importance of confidentiality	Governing board members and/or Campaign director
5.	Role of the steering committee A. Worker assignments B. Training and assignment meeting (dates and times)	Chairperson
6.	Questions, concerns	Participants
7.	Achieving campaign goal A. The challenge	Campaign director
8.	Closing prayer	

---

6. What questions should be asked if a school wants to establish an educational endowment fund?

Do the parish leaders support the establishment of an educational endowment fund? Is it the right time to establish an endowment fund governing board? Is it time to promote aggressively the endowment fund as an identifiable entity? Should a budget for clerical support of ongoing endowment fund activities be established? How should these changes be implemented? If all these questions are answered affirmatively, then you are ready to start the process.

7. How do you start the process of establishing an educational endowment?

Establish a volunteer group to develop a brochure describing the education fund. The group should be staffed with people likely to become the first governing board. The most important part of the brochure is the case statement for the endowment fund. Start an alumni liaison activity. Find a person to start setting up linkages between alumni and the school, such as an alumni news journal. Start team activities with parish groups, especially those that develop linkages with new people in the community and with the faculty, to keep them informed as to what is happening and establish a consensus to determine activities to take place in the school. Get area high schools and colleges to act as sources of information about the activities of the alumni. See the sample timeline that follows.

SAMPLE TIMELINE FOR ESTABLISHING AN EDUCATIONAL ENDOWMENT

January	Review and discuss endowment fund governing board recommendations. (The governing board should be made up of six or seven select, qualified members with knowledge in financial matters and public relations, and they must be team players.)
April	Report to the parish regarding endowment study. Create long-range planning task force (5 to 10 members). Initiate review of legal documents to create endowment.
May	Initiate communications plan with first issue of quarterly newsletter. Develop bulletin announcements related to gifting beyond lifetime. Continue review of legal documents to create endowment. Have long-range planning task force under way.
June	Complete legal documents to create endowment. Develop endowment education brochure.
August	Continue newsletter communication.
September	Continue long-range planning task force activity. Continue endowment education efforts through will awareness and financial planning seminars.
October	Have long-range task force issue interim report.
November	Continue newsletter communication. Encourage year-end giving through education efforts.
December	Evaluate plan of action for adjustments and changes.

See Worksheet 10.1 at the end of this chapter for a sample checklist of the various campaign activities; see sample pledge card in Worksheet 10.2.

8. What results can a school expect in the first year's efforts?

The results to expect within the first year are the establishment of a governing board, the establishment of an alumni liaison function, and the establishment of a school development-marketing program. The function of a development-marketing program is to find ways for the school to be made known, to tell its story to the wider parish and beyond-parish communities. An excellent medium is a video about 6-10 minutes long to be used as part of the endowment program presentation. The video may also be used in a variety of ways to help the school, such as for recruiting potential new parents, engaging alumni in the development program, and sharing with the local media.

(Gary G. Wilmer, M.S., is principal of St. Charles Borromeo School in Minneapolis, Minnesota.)

WORKSHEET 10.1

Campaign Activity Checklist

(This list includes suggested terms, preceded by an asterisk, to be used in a timetable for the different activities.)

ACTIVITY	STATUS	DATE COMPLETED
Presentation Booklet (Past, present, future of school)	*Printed	_____
Video Presentation	*Produced	_____
Dates for Breakfast Focus-Group Meetings	*Initiated	_____
Presentations of Videotaped and Verbal Explanation of Endowment	*Finished	_____
Determination of Major Prospects	*Drafted	_____
Organizational Chart	*Drafted	_____
Leadership Job Description	*Drafted	_____
Design for Campaign Theme	*Initiated	_____
Campaign Leadership Team	*Initiated	_____
Videotapes for Leadership	*Ordered	_____
Dates for Community Meetings	*Initiated	_____

WORKSHEET 10.2

Pledge Card

Pledge Card

Phase I

$_____$ Total Gift

$_____$ Down Payment

$_____$ Balance Due

Please remind me of this 36-month commitment:

_____monthly   _____quarterly

_____semiannually   _____annually

Phase II

_____YES, I/we will make a planned gift in the form of a bequest, annuity, insurance policy, trust, or other deferred gift of $10,000 or more naming **The Church of**_____ **Catholic Education Endowment** as the beneficiary of the gift.

Signature_____

Date_____

All gifts are fully tax-deductible, as provided by current law.

Thank you for pledging your support.

CHAPTER 11:
GRANT WRITING

Jim Brennan

This chapter will answer these questions:
1. What is grant writing?
2. Why should your school get involved in grant writing?
3. What is some preparatory work that must be done before beginning to write a grant proposal?
4. What are the four steps in the process of grant writing?
5. Who should do the grant writing?

1. What is grant writing?

Grant writing seeks out funding from a foundation for a specific purpose. Grant writing can be a powerful means to secure funds for a school. All too often, however, it is looked upon either as something too complicated or as something only highly trained professionals can do. Although both of these points may have their merit, the process of requesting funds from foundations should not be abandoned. A certain degree of success can be attained with appropriate information and a realistic understanding of the process.

2. Why should your school get involved in grant writing?

"Catholic School Awarded $500,000 Grant!" Wouldn't that be great, if that were a headline about your school? It is happening more and more, perhaps not for that great an amount of money, but it does happen. So, why let it always be the other school? Why not get involved in the process so that one day it could be a headline of a success story about your school?

3. What is some preparatory work that must be done before attempting to write a grant proposal?

Does your school already have a clearly defined mission statement? If not, start here. What is your school's mission statement? Of all its goals and objectives, cite one that will be the focus of your request to a foundation. A sample of the statement we used for our school is presented on the following page.

At the end of this chapter, you will find Worksheet 11.1, Beginning a Grant Proposal, which will provide you with a sample of how you can identify who you are as a school (the mission statement); what you want your students to be able to do (one goal and supporting objectives); and what you see as important to support their development in this area (resources needed). Please note that this worksheet is not a grant proposal; it is just preliminary work or organized notes for the writer to begin to focus on necessary research before beginning the proposal. Use this sample as a guide to begin to process a worksheet for your school. Take time to reflect on the mission statement, one prioritized goal to support the mission, and then on the resources that would enhance and promote your efforts to achieve it.

SAMPLE MISSION STATEMENT: HOLY SPIRIT SCHOOL

Holy Spirit School's mission is to create a Christian educational community where human culture and knowledge, enlightened and enlivened by faith, are shared in a spirit of love.

Specific Goal and Objectives of Holy Spirit School
It is the goal of Holy Spirit School to enable its students not only to be computer literate but also to be intelligent users of modern technology. This will be achieved through providing the students with—

1. A regular program of instruction in the area of technology
2. Opportunities to utilize technology as a support for learning in the content areas of the curriculum
3. An awareness and experience that demonstrates that technology is a means to communication, information, and understanding, with the known world as the school house

Resources Needed to Support These Objectives:

1. A fully equipped computer laboratory for daily student instruction
2. Teacher workstations for the computer lab and each classroom
3. Four student workstations in each classroom
4. Internet access for all workstations

---

4. What are the four steps in the process of grant writing?

The following four steps will provide the new grant writer with some initial direction and insight into the process of writing grant proposals:

- Define the identified need for your grant proposal
- Identify foundations that match your identified need
- Understand the basic components of a grant proposal
- Develop an action plan for soliciting funds through grant proposals

Step 1: Define the identified need for your grant proposal. Now it may seem rather evident that if you are going to be successful in asking for something, you need to know what you want. This cannot be overemphasized. If what you want is not exactly crystal clear to you, then it will not be clear to those who review your grant proposal. An example of a need that is not crystal clear or specific is to say that you need funds to pay for general operating expenses.

Being painstakingly clear about what you want is only part of the task. You need to be able to identify how the proposed grant will support your school's purpose. You need to show a very clear understanding of what your school is about. This typically is reflected in a mission statement and made more specific in the goals and objectives of your school.

What is necessary, therefore, is not just a desire to acquire more resources for your school but an understanding of what your school's goals and objectives are and how they will be enhanced through the granting of the funds that you are requesting.

Step 2: Identify foundations that match your identified need. Once you have begun to focus your grant by using Worksheet 11.1 in this chapter, you can start to consider the foundations from which you will seek your resources. It is important to match up your identified need with a foundation that is interested in funding your type of project.

Many foundations limit their giving to a particular state or region. Foundation books (available at your local public library) list what foundations will fund and what they will not fund. If a foundation requirement is that funding will be given only to health-related projects in the state of Illinois, and you live in New York, do not waste your time approaching that foundation. Foundation books also list average funding given to projects that foundations accept or the limit they will give. You need to know all this from the outset.

When you start searching out the foundations that will match your need, take note of what their preferences in giving are. Some variables to consider are geographic location, size of project, amount of money (resources) requested, level of education funded (e.g., primary versus secondary education), special-interest groups targeted for grants, and other special conditions. Below is a sample sheet used by Holy Spirit School, to help you prepare for the search.

SAMPLE PREPARATORY SHEET FOR FOUNDATION SEARCH

1. Project objective summary - Obtain additional computer hardware and software for computer lab

2. Type of resources needed - Money or in-kind donations

3. Amount of resources needed - Minimum $20,000 purchasing power to equip computer lab

4. Location of the project - United States
   Northern California
   San Francisco Bay Area

5. Special-interest field - Computer technology
   Computer education

6. Education level of project - Elementary education (K-8)

7. Type of sponsoring agent - Nonprofit
   Religious/Catholic
   Elementary school

8. Timeline - Implementation by September 1

Step 3 : Understand the basic components of a grant proposal. You have now begun to identify the project that you will request to be supported by foundations. You have furthermore attempted to identify the significant characteristics of your proposed project and have matched your need to those identified by foundations in the various foundation books as ones they want to support. Basically, you need to find the clearest match as possible between your school and a foundation that wants to fund your type of project. It is not necessarily easy, but it should be clear and possible with concerted effort. Worksheet 11.2 at the end of this chapter will help you organize this information.

To establish a need that a foundation wants to fund, you must begin to tell your story in the manner that the foundation wants to hear it. Not all foundations want the story told the same way, but there are some consistent components of the story that you can prepare that may be applicable to a variety of foundations. You need to understand these components and their purpose in order to help you tell your story in a way that the foundation will "buy it." Note that some foundations have specific forms to be filled out to request funding. Foundation books will have this information, and your first step might be to write to the foundation to ask for proposal forms.

Grant proposals have specific parts:

(a) For the first part, write an introduction, which will be a brief overview of the proposal. It should be fairly short and able to attract interest so that the reader will want to examine the details of the grant.

(b) For the second part of the proposal, write a needs assessment. A background of your school is essential and so are the events that have led to the necessity for the project and why you are applying.

(c) In the next part, identify the objective and activities that will help you achieve your goal. Tell what you are going to do and why. This should be very clearly linked to the goal; results should be measurable.

(d) In the next section, include a timeline, which is needed information on when the activity or project will happen. Illustrate that the project is achievable and give an appropriate time frame.

(e) In the next section, discuss money for the project. Describe the fiscal requirements of your project. Identify the necessary income and expense categories. An overview of the budget is helpful.

(f) Lastly, promise an evaluation after the project is completed. At that time, you will illustrate how you accomplished your goal through the achievement of your objectives. Gather data all along the way: bills for items needed, installation costs, etc., and state the significant positive impact on the school because of this achievement. Worksheet 11.3 at the end of this chapter provides an outline for a typical proposal; fill it in before you begin the actual writing.

Step 4: Develop an action plan for soliciting funds through grant proposals. Grant proposals do not just happen. Planning and preparation are needed if the project is going to have a chance to be successful. This planning calls the principal or grant writer to have a clear idea of what is going to be done, when it will be done, and what is expected to be the outcome of the actions. Specified action plans will not guarantee success, but they will help identify exactly what needs to be done and when this should be accomplished.

You will notice that the three preceding goals involve gathering information in preparation for developing the action plan. The action plan then is to put the pieces together in an organized fashion. Once you have organized and carried out your action plan, you should be ready to write your proposal. You might be thinking, "After all this work, I'm only ready to begin writing my proposal?" Although it may seem like a lot of work to get to this point, because of preparation such as this, your proposal writing should be more specific, take less time, and hopefully be more successful.

At this point you should refer to *Grant Proposals: A Primer for Writers*, published by NCEA (1994), to take you to the next step in the completion of your proposal-writing activities.

5. Who should do the grant writing?

If your school is fortunate enough to have a development officer, of course that person should write the proposal. If your school is just beginning, below is a sample process you can use to help you prepare to write the grant. This sample is intended to provide a framework from which to work once you have decided to write the proposal. Before writing the grant, however, you will need to obtain an application from the funding source and follow the specific guidelines given.

SAMPLE PREPARATORY PROCESS FOR WRITING A GRANT

Activity	Lead person	Timeline	Outcome
Review of mission statement (Worksheet 11.1)	Principal	August faculty meeting	Reaffirmed mission statement
Agree on this year's goal (Worksheet 11.1)	Principal	August faculty meeting	Priorities set
Develop objectives to support goal (Worksheet 11.1)	Principal	September 7th faculty meeting	Activities identified to support objectives
Identify resources needed (Worksheet 11.1)	Principal	September 7th faculty meeting	Specific resources identified
Research funding sources (Worksheet 11.2)	Faculty Chairperson	October 1st	Foundations targeted for requests
Prepare information for funding sources (Worksheet 11.3)	Faculty Chairperson	October 1st	Necessary proposal information prepared

You need to complete Worksheet 11.4, at the end of this chapter, for your situation.

The worksheets that follow are not intended to help writers produce a final copy of a grant proposal, but rather to provide time for reflection and brainstorming as the writers of the proposal begin to get specific and earnest about their intentions.

(Jim Brennan, Ed.D., is an assistant superintendent of schools for the Diocese of San Jose in California. The information in this chapter was gathered while he was principal of Holy Spirit School in the Diocese of Oakland.)

Additional Reading on the Topic from NCEA

Mathis, Emily D., and Doody, John E. (1994). *Grant Proposals: A Primer for Writers.*

WORKSHEET 11.1

Beginning a Grant Proposal

School _____ Date_____

1. Mission Statement

   _____

   _____

   _____

   _____

   _____

2. Specific Goal

   _____

   _____

   _____

   _____

   Objectives

   A._____

   _____

   B. _____

   _____

   C._____

   _____

3. Resources Needed to Support These Objectives

   _____

   _____

   _____

WORKSHEET 11.2

Identifying the Right Foundation

1. Project Objective Summary

   _____

   _____

2. Type of Resources Needed

   _____

   _____

3. Amount of Resources Needed

   _____

   _____

4. Location of the Project

   _____

   _____

5. Special-Interest Field

   _____

   _____

6. Education Level of Project

   _____

   _____

7. Type of Sponsoring Group

   _____

   _____

8. Timeline

   _____

   _____

9. Other Distinguishing Characteristics

   _____

   _____

WORKSHEET 11.3

Preparing to Write the Grant Proposal

1. Introduction

   _____

   _____

   _____

   _____

2. Program/Description

   _____

   _____

   _____

   _____

3. Needs Assessment

   _____

   _____

   _____

   _____

4. Objectives

   _____

   _____

   _____

5. Timeline

   _____

   _____

   _____

6. Budget

   _____

   _____

   _____

7. Evaluation

   _____

   _____

   _____

WORKSHEET 11.4

Preparing a Specific Action Plan

Activity	Lead Person	Timeline	Outcome
1.			
2.			
3.			
4.			
5.			
6.			
7.			
8.			

CHAPTER 12:
ANNUAL REPORT

Sister Joseph Spring, SCC, and James Cassidy

This chapter will answer these questions:

1. What is an annual report?
2. Who prepares the annual report?
3. How is an annual report prepared?
4. What is contained in an annual report?
5. Who is the annual report audience?
6. When is the annual report written and distributed?
7. Why an annual report?

1. What is an annual report?

An annual report is simply what it states: annual report. An annual report is an effective tool to report to the school/parish community the various accomplishments of the school, its vision for the future, and its financial status. Issued each year at a set time, it gives the school community a sense of accomplishment and a perception that their achievements have been recognized. It is also an effective marketing tool that can be given to those who are unfamiliar with the school.

2. Who prepares the annual report?

The school's development committee or educational council take responsibility for the production of the document. It can be as simple as a tri-fold brochure or as elaborate as a 25-page report.

The school pastor and principal should be assigned a prominent role in the writing. An open letter to the readers is an appropriate topic for the pastor. The principal can give an update on the educational programs offered and the status of any statewide or regional accreditation process. For instance, our school, St. Joseph School in Mendham, New Jersey, must give a three-year progress report to the Middle States Association of Schools and Colleges. Part of the reporting protocol is making public to the school community the progress on the school's goals. The annual report becomes an effective vehicle for that reporting.

3. How is an annual report prepared?

It is better if one person assumes the task of writing the report, except for the letters of the pastor and principal, after the information has been collected from the various committee members. One person writing the text provides continuity and the sense of a single author. The author should be someone with firsthand knowledge of the school, so that what is stated is reported clearly and accurately.

The annual report can be professionally composed on desktop publishing, such as Microsoft Publishing or PageMaker. Both programs provide a suggested format for the report, and the same format can be saved from year to year and the appropriate information updated. Depending upon the look you want to achieve and the number of copies needed, the printed text can then be sent to a printer for reproduction or it can be duplicated locally.

The end product should truly represent the character of the school. It should be neat, attractive, and professional looking. It should not be extravagant (e.g., glossy, multicolored text) unless this is the image the school wishes to project. Pictures, graphs, little boxes of text, inspirational sayings, and quotes from students break the monotony of the solid text and present an interesting and inviting appearance.

4. What is contained in an annual report?

Just to give you an idea, below is the format our school, St. Joseph's in Mendham, New Jersey, has effectively used in its annual report. The topics, the content, and the person responsible or the source for the information (in parenthesis) are indicated.

(a) **Open letter (pastor)** - The pastor reiterates his commitment to Catholic education in the parish and reflects on the quality of education being offered in the school. His letter establishes a nice tone for the report.

(b) **Mission statement (taken from the school philosophy)** - For those unfamiliar with the school, this section presents the driving purpose, the raison d'etre, of the school.

(c) **Catholic Schools Week (principal)** - In this part of the report, the principal states the national theme set by the National Catholic Educational Association and describes how the school incorporates that theme into the yearlong celebration as well as the Catholic Schools Week celebration. This shows the link between the school and the national office.

(d) **Spiritual life of the school (principal)** - One of the goals our school has set is "to secure the ongoing Catholicity of the school." This section is the report to the school/parish community of how the school implements that goal during the course of the year.

(e) **Programs and activities (principal)** - Another goal that our school has set is "to implement the whole language program in the school." This section highlights how the school works toward achieving that goal during the year.

(f) **Field trips (teacher)** - This section lists the cultural opportunities the children are afforded through field trips during the year.

(g) **Volunteers (HSA president)** - The volunteer opportunities in the school are listed and described. This list shows parents, especially those new to the school, how they can get more involved in the life of the school. It serves the school well, since it recruits new volunteers. It also provides a public opportunity to thank those who have so generously given of their time and talent.

(h) **Faculty accomplishments (principal)** - This highlights faculty members' awards received, courses of study completed, and projects recognized and the workshops they have attended. Faculty are listed with their degrees and the colleges/universities that conferred the degrees.

(i) **Student awards and academic achievements (principal)** - This material is collected throughout the year and reported again at the end. In the case of St. Joseph's School, it also summarizes how well the students of the school did on the current standardized testing.

(j) **Sports (coaches)** - The coaches of the various teams highlight their accomplishments for the season. Again, this is an opportunity to show the breadth of the school's programs.

(k) **Tuition and finances (finance chairperson)** - New tuition and fees are listed. A full financial report of the school is presented, including a graph that shows income and expenditures by category. This section is also used to show what percentage of operating costs came from tuition, from parish subsidy, and from fund-raising.

(l) **Fund-raising (HSA president)** - This part of the report names and describes the fund-raisers, indicating cost and the financial profit to the school. It serves to inform new families of the nature of the events, so that they can get involved.

(m) **Alumni (chair of the alumni association)** - A summary of alumni events for the past year is reported.

(n) **Education council and HSA executive board (chair of the council)** - A listing of the members of these two very important groups is provided.

(o) **Spotlight on... (education council)** - Each year, a group or individual, e.g., sports team, volunteers, principal, teacher, is "spotlighted." This makes the report somewhat personal and ends the report with a strong motivation to continue to support the school.

5.   Who is the annual report audience?

The annual report is written primarily for the school and parish community. It is a document for the constituency. It is distributed to each school family in the weekly family envelope, to parishioners as a Sunday bulletin insert, to the faculty and staff, to alumni, to local businesses, and to other interested parties. It well serves the purpose, however, of a marketing tool and a vehicle of introduction to the school for prospective students/families.

6.   When is the annual report written and distributed?

As can be seen from the topics covered, many of the sections can be written well before the end of the year. Some, however, cannot be finished until the school year is completed. From experience, we can say, "Be sure all information is handed to you before the summer break. You will never get it once school is out!"

Sufficient lead time must be allowed to collect the information from the assigned committee members, to compose text, to type text into the computer, and, finally and probably most important, to proofread, edit, and proofread again. This document will represent your school, so you want it to be letter-perfect.

A suitable distribution time is either at the conclusion of the current school year or at the beginning of the new school year. You may find it more workable (we did) to issue it at the beginning of the new school year, since at that point the school community's interest is peaked and you have an eager audience. It also serves the purpose of giving the group time over the summer to write, collate, assemble, and print the document.

7.   Why an annual report?

At this point, you can answer this question. The annual report is a document of the school, by the school, for the school. It is a "brag book," a record of events, a marketing tool. It establishes the school's credibility in the larger community. Each school should be proud to record and publish its story annually.

(Sister Joseph Spring, SCC, M.A., was principal of St. Joseph School in Mendham, New Jersey, at the time of this writing. Currently, she is principal of St. Mary School in Hackettstown, New Jersey. This chapter is coauthored by James Cassidy, an education council member for St. Joseph School.)

Additional Reading on the Topic from NCEA

Donaldson, Frank. (1991). *Catholic School Publications: Unifying the Image.*

WORKSHEET 12.1

Timeline for Annual Report Production

DATE	TASK
_____	Assemble the committee to write annual report
	Checklist:
	_____ Distribute topics
	_____ Set deadlines
	_____ Determine editing responsibilities
	_____ Secure printer
	_____ Determine audience for distribution
_____	Submit working copy to editor
_____	Return final draft to committee for approval
_____	Take document to printer
_____	Distribute document to targeted audiences

WORKSHEET 12.2

Assignments for Annual Report

TOPIC	PERSON RESPONSIBLE
Open Letter	_____
Mission Statement	_____
Catholic Schools Week	_____
Spiritual Life of the School	_____
Programs and Activities	_____
Field Trips	_____
Volunteers	_____
Faculty Accomplishments	_____
Student Awards and Academic Achievements	_____
Sports	_____
Tuition and Finances	_____
Fund-raising	_____
Alumni	_____
Education Council/HSA Executive Board	_____
Spotlight on . . .	_____